make
music now!

Edited by Mitch Gallagher

Backbeat
Books

San Francisco

Published by Backbeat Books
600 Harrison Street, San Francisco, CA 94107
E-mail: books@musicplayer.com
www.backbeatbooks.com
An imprint of the Music Player Network
United Entertainment Media

Distributed to the book trade in the US and Canada by
Publishers Group West, 1700 Fourth Street, Berkeley, CA 94710

Distributed to the music trade in the US and Canada by
Hal Leonard Publishing, P.O. Box 13819, Milwaukee, WI 53213

Cover Design by Richard Leeds
Text Design and Composition by Greene Design
Front Cover Design and Illustration by John Ueland

Printed in the United States of America

Library of Congress Cataloging-in-Publication Data

Gallagher, Mitch
       Make music now! / Mitch Gallagher
             p. cm.
       ISBN 0-87930-637-8
       1. Music—Data processing. 2. Sound—Recording and reproducing.
3. Sound studios—Equipment and supplies. 4. Computer sound processing.
I. Title.

MT723.G35 2002
621.389'3—dc21   2002016090

02 03 04 05 06   5 4 3 2 1

table of contents

ACKNOWLEDGMENTS

Sometimes a project, such as a book like this, can seem like a solo endeavor, but that's rarely the case. It's impossible to do such a work without the support and inspiration of many people. I'd like to pass on my thanks to those who helped me out—whether they know it or not!

Thank you to:

My family and friends, Jim Aikin, Doug Beck, Jim Bordner, Scott Garrigus, Rob McGaughey, Greg Rule, and the staffs at *Keyboard* and *EQ* magazines.

Special thanks to:

Marvin Sanders, who took a chance and gave me my journalistic shot at *Keyboard*.

Richard Johnston and the staff at Backbeat Books, who endured numerous missed deadlines (sorry 'bout that!).

Mom and Dad, who uncomplainingly supported my forays into music from Day One.

Once upon a time, it wasn't a simple matter to put together a decent home studio if you didn't have a substantial budget to work with. Most of the "affordable" gear available at the time was up to the demands of recording demos, but really couldn't claim to be able to produce "master quality" recordings.

Fortunately, things have come a long, long way since then. With the digital and home computer revolutions have come unprecedented power and capabilities at even more unprecedented prices. I remember my first "home studio." It was around 20 years ago. (No, I'm not that old; I was just really young at the time....) I had just returned to college to study music after spending several years touring the Midwestern United States as a guitarist with various and sundry rock and country-rock acts. The university I chose to attend had a small recording studio and a couple of electronic music labs, but I quickly grew tired of not being able to use them whenever I wanted—sharing those resources with other students was a drag. Plus, I just never seemed to be able to come up with cool ideas in those rooms the way that I could when I was sitting comfortably at home strumming my guitar in front of the television.

A short time before this, I had traded my brother a leather motorcycle jacket for his Commodore 64 computer, and had scrimped and saved to purchase a small Yamaha drum machine that I used for practicing guitar. I also owned a six-channel powered PA mixer and a pair of small Radio Shack PA speakers (can't remember how I ended up with *those* beauties). With the help of my parents, I was able to acquire a Yamaha DX100 and a Casio CZ101—both small digital synthesizers that featured those unplayable "mini" keys instead of full-sized, piano-style keys. I also scored a 360 Systems MIDI Bass, which was a small monophonic MIDI module that played eight-bit samples of real basses; amazing for that day and age. A local music store gave me a MIDI interface for the Commodore 64 and a copy of some long-gone, very primitive sequencer program; this was in the early days of MIDI and they had no idea what to do with those items so they donated them to me. For mixdown, I used the cassette deck from my home stereo.

Looking back, it sounds like an extremely rag-tag collection of bargain basement gear—and it was! But I created a pile of music using that rig, and had an absolute blast doing it. Occasionally, I'd pack all that stuff up and lug it over to the university's studio so that I could record guitars and vocals along with my synth-generated tracks. But most of my work was done right there in front of that rig in a corner of my living room, writing music, trying ideas, and learning a tremendous amount about the gear and the recording process.

My little pile of cheap gear served as the basis for an ever-improving, ever-expanding studio that, over the years, evolved into a full-on, professional recording studio capable of sound quality that rivals that produced in the largest state-of-the-art commercial studios.

But all that took place in the last millennium. These days, for the money I spent on that original home studio, you could put together a rig that would be so much more powerful, so much more capable, and sound so much better, that there wouldn't be any comparison between the two. In fact, if you're just getting into the home studio game, you couldn't have come along at a better time. Prices are way down, and features and sound quality are the best they've ever been. For most of us, the gear is no longer the defining factor in achieving good sound quality—even the least expensive audio products sound fine. Rather, it's your skill as a musician, engineer, and producer that will determine how good you sound. And in a home studio environment, you're ideally set up to spend as much time and effort as you want or have available on sounding good. You have the freedom to work on your music as much or as little as you choose. This is a tremendous benefit that's really only become available to us in recent years. Once you've bought the gear, it doesn't cost you a cent to spend more time working on a song or idea. (Okay, so you might spend a few pennies for electricity and for a blank tape or CD-R disc now and then, but run with me; I'm trying to make a point here....)

But let's not forget: Owning a home studio isn't necessarily about becoming a great engineer or producer, it's about having the tools to create the music you want to create. That's the key; the goal to keep in mind—it's all about making music. Thus the title of this book: *Make Music Now!* It's so easy to get distracted by technology and technique, but all the gear and effort in the world won't mean a thing if you don't keep the focus tight on making music. So spend as much time as you need learning to use you studio as well as you can, but don't forget why you're really there.

Putting together a home studio and using it to create and record music, whether your own or someone else's, is one of the most rewarding and fun things you can do. There's simply nothing like the feeling you get when you sit down to listen to a recording of music you've made with your own two hands and your own heart and mind. So what are you waiting for? Let's get in there and make music now! —*Mitch Gallagher*

About MAKE MUSIC NOW!

This book has been organized into three sections, each of which focuses on a particular aspect of making music in a home studio. You'll get the most out of *Make Music Now!* if you sit down and read it through. But the book's been designed so that each chapter stands on its own, so if there's a particular topic that you feel the need to explore right now, go ahead and jump straight to it—you won't hurt my feelings! Here's the way things are laid out:

PART ONE—THE BASICS. You can't build a house without a strong foundation, and you can't get the most out of a home studio without understanding a few basics. Part One will be the foundation we build our studios on.

Chapter 1—The Basics of Sound. In this chapter we'll discuss the basics of sound and audio, define some important terms you'll need, and lay out the concepts necessary for understanding how a studio works.

Chapter 2—Ones and Zeros. These days, pretty much everything we'll deal with in our home studios will end up as digital audio at one point or another. Chapter Two is where we'll dig into the meat of how digital audio works, learning along the way how to get the most out of a digital system. Don't worry, it'll be painless!

Chapter 3—Making Music with MIDI. Unless you're working with purely acoustic music, at some point or another you'll probably need to put MIDI to work for you. We've got the lowdown on how to do it, simply and easily.

PART TWO—PUTTING YOUR STUDIO TOGETHER. This section will help you figure out the what, why, and how behind assembling a home studio—no matter what your budget!

Chapter 4—Guide to Studio Equipment. Don't know a microphone from a megaphone? No worries! Chapter Four will take you on a tour of all the hardware that you'll need to make your studio fly.

Chapter 5—Who's Afraid of Hard Disk? These days, personal computers, whether Macs or PCs, are the centerpieces in most studios. This chapter will guide you through what you need to turn your computer into a studio powerhouse.

Chapter 6—Choosing a Computer. Not sure if your old computer can keep up with the demands of digital recording and MIDI? Chapter Six spells out exactly how much computer you'll need so you can shop or upgrade with confidence.

Chapter 7—Software for the Studio. So you've got the perfect computer for your studio. Now what? Without the right software, it ain't going nowhere! In this chapter you'll learn about the different types of audio and music programs and which ones you'll need to make your music.

Chapter 8—Plug-In! In days gone by, you needed racks and racks of expensive equipment in order to create good-sounding tracks. But that's all changed in today's digital world, where software rules. Nowhere is this more evident than with plug-ins, inexpensive little programs that replace all types of hardware boxes.

Chapter 9—Freeware and Shareware. Need to stretch your home-studio dollar to the absolute limit? This chapter will show you how, by using free and super-inexpensive software to replace expensive "commercial" programs.

Chapter 10—Microphone Basics. Whether you're recording vocals or acoustic instruments, choosing and using the right microphone is key to great results.

Chapter 11—Improving Your Studio's Acoustics. The acoustics in your studio play a vital role in the final sound of your recordings. Whether your studio is in a guest bedroom, the basement, the garage, or a corner of the living room, here's how to give it a complete acoustic makeover.

Chapter 12 —Working Efficiently. Wish you had more time to spend on your music? Chapter 12 is filled with suggestions for cutting down on wasted studio time, so that you can spend as much time as possible where it counts: making music!

Chapter 13—Combating Silence. It's inevitable. Sooner or later you're going to have to solve a gear, computer, or software problem in your home studio. No fear! Chapter 13 has the information you'll need to do it quickly, easily, and without unnecessary suffering so you can get back to creating music.

PART THREE—MAKE MUSIC NOW! This part of the book is where we really get into what's important: how to use your home studio to create and record your musical visions. Clear a spot on the mantel for your Grammy!

Chapter 14—Recording a Song in Seven Easy Steps. Have a pile great song ideas, but not sure how to get them recorded? Chapter 14 will guide you, step-by-step, through the process of creating, demoing, tracking, and mixing your masterpiece.

Chapter 15—Crafting Soundscape. No one is going to want to listen to your musical gems if they don't sound their best. This chapter will help you craft and polish your ideas until they shine like the diamonds they are.

Chapter 16—Recording Yourself. Working alone in your studio? Flying solo can be both a blessing and a curse. Here's how to stay on track when recording and producing yourself.

Chapter 17—Remixing 101. Remixing is one of the hottest areas of music production today; just check out the music being played in any dance club. Chapter 17 will show you how to get started remixing right now!

Chapter 18—Making Loop-based Music. The use of loops (short repeating snippets of audio that are assembled to form a song) in today's music is running rampant. Here's how to get in on the fun. It's easy, it's fast, and Chapter 18 will show you how to do it the right way.

Chapter 19—Ten Ways to Enjoy Your Studio. So you've gathered the gear, set it up in an acoustically wonderful room, and you have it all working the way it's supposed to. Now what do you do with it? You'll find ten great ideas for things you can do with your studio in this chapter. We'll even show you how to make a few bucks with your home studio!

Chapter 20—Putting Your Music Online. For independent (and not-so-independent) musicians, the Internet has become one of the primary means of getting music heard. If you're looking for a guide to getting your music on the Web, this chapter has it.

Chapter 21—Creating Your Own Audio CDs. Once upon a time you could get away with putting out your music on a hand-labeled cassette. These days, if you want to be taken seriously, you need a CD of your tunes. Fortunately, putting your music on disc is a quick and easy task—especially after you've read this chapter.

Chapter 22—Preparing Your CD for Replication. Ready to take your musical masterpiece to the next level? Thousands of rabid fans clamoring to buy your latest disc? You need the services of a CD replicator, who will duplicate and package your disc. This chapter provides the secrets to getting the best deal and the best results from your replicator.

Glossary. Closing out *Make Music Now!* is the Glossary, an extensive collection of the terms and definitions you'll encounter on your journey to Home Studio Nirvana.

an introduction to the basics

the basics of sound

BY MITCH GALLAGHER

t o state the completely obvious, almost all audio recordings must start with sound, so it makes sense for us to start our journey into putting together a home studio and putting it to use creating music by exploring just a bit of science behind sound itself. Don't worry, we're not after a physicist's or acoustician's understanding of the topic, just a basic grasp of the fundamentals and some of the common terms you're going to encounter over and over again in your music-making life.

Sound Waves, Frequency, and Pitch

Sound waves are just what their name implies, actual wave motion or vibration, similar to ocean waves, moving through the air. The sound waves create pressure differences inside our ears, which our brain converts into what we recognize as "sound." These pressure changes occur at different rates, which we call frequencies. Frequency is the number of wave crests (vibrations) that occur in a given period of time, usually a second. Each passing crest of a wave is called a cycle, thus the term "cycles per second," or Hertz (Hz), named for the man who did research into sound waves. You'll often see or hear the term "kiloHertz" (kHz), which represents a unit of one thousand Hertz or cycles per second. So, for example, 10kHz equals 10,000Hz.

Frequency determines the musical pitch of a tone; for example, a common tuning reference for musicians is "A440"—where the note "A" has a frequency of 440Hz. A musical octave is a doubling of frequency, so the A an octave above A440 would be at 880Hz, the next octave above at 1,760Hz (1.76kHz), and so on.

The generally accepted range of frequencies humans can hear is approximately 20Hz to 20kHz (20,000Hz), depending on the age of the listener and how much loud noise the ears have been exposed to. As we age or are exposed to loud noises, we tend to lose high-frequency response in our ears. You can break down the human range of hearing very roughly as follows:

Frequency	Instruments and characteristics
10–80Hz	Lower bass, kick drum, bass synth, rumble, richness, power, thump
80–200Hz	Upper bass, bass instruments, rhythm section, lower guitar range
200–500Hz	Lower midrange, rhythm and accompaniment instruments
500Hz–2.5kHz	Midrange, violin, piano, solo instruments, vocals
2.5–5kHz	Upper midrange, harmonics and overtones, brightness
5–10kHz	Lower treble, hiss, presence, shimmer
10–20kHz	Upper treble, sheen, liveness, air

A good understanding of frequencies, their relationship to musical notes, and the area of the human range of hearing they occupy can be of great help when it comes time to equalize (EQ) or adjust the tone of a sound, recorded track, or mix.

Wavelength

Wavelength is quite literally the physical measure of how long a particular sound wave is—a low note or bass tone may be many feet long, while a high frequency may be only a few inches long. For most audio applications, this isn't a big concern, but it does become important when dealing with room acoustics, phase, and in microphone applications.

Waveform

The waveform, or shape, of a sound wave determines its "timbre" or tonal quality. Almost no sounds are made up of just a single frequency; rather, a sound is normally composed of a complex array of frequencies, with the base frequency called the fundamental, and those above it referred to as harmonics or overtones. The harmonic spectrum, or collection of overtones that make up a sound, is what gives it a unique sound—what makes a trumpet sound different from a violin.

Frequency Response

A frequency-response measurement or specification is a description of the ability of a piece of audio gear to pass or reproduce the full range of audio frequencies. Flat frequency response, or the ability of a piece of equipment to reproduce all the frequencies sent to it equally well, is especially desirable in many types of audio gear. However, in many cases, gear is designed *not* to have completely flat frequency response. For example, a microphone might have a slight boost in the upper midrange frequencies to give a vocal track more presence in a mix. Other pieces of gear are designed to have a "warm" sound, with less flat response in the upper frequencies.

In the past, frequency response from 20Hz to 20kHz was considered adequate. However, with the arrival of new digital delivery mediums such as DVD and SACD, top-end frequency responses have increased radically to 96kHz and even higher.

As with all gear specifications, frequency response shouldn't be taken as the be-all, end-all. It's just one part of the equation. Nor should you be overly concerned with manufacturers' claims of "flat" frequency responses. As an example, virtually every studio speaker manufacturer claims that their monitors have ruler-flat frequency response. Yet somehow each monitor has a unique sound. In the end, the best measure of any piece of gear is how it sounds to your ears.

Decibels

The term decibel, or dB, is one that you'll encounter constantly in your studio. Like most terms and measurements used in the audio field, it was developed and defined by the telephone industry, and in fact, was named for Alexander Graham Bell. Simply put, the decibel is a ratio between the strength of two signals. Because of the way our ears work and the extremely wide range of loudness levels they can deal with, the decibel is based on a logarithmic, rather than a linear, scale of measurement.

A decibel specification may be above or below a given reference. Microphones, for example, are generally rated below a given standard; a particular model may be rated at –60dB, or 60dB below a given zero reference.

In acoustic terms, the smallest change most people can perceive without a reference is around 1dB, but in the context of a mix, engineers can often hear changes as small as 0.1dB.

It's worth it to pick up an inexpensive decibel monitor and to keep it handy in your studio. (Radio Shack sells two appropriate models.) Prolonged exposure to high decibel levels can cause hearing damage, plus, the frequency response of our ears changes depending on volume and time of exposure—when mixing music, most engineers work in the range of 85dB, dropping to lower levels and cranking up to slightly higher levels occasionally to double-check their work.

Dynamic Range

Dynamic range is a measurement of the difference between the softest and loudest signals a piece of audio gear will deal with, or more accurately, the difference between the noise floor—the level of background noise a piece of gear produces—and the onset of distortion. Distortion can be defined as an unwanted change in the character of an audio signal. Typically this appears as clipping, where the level of the signal exceeds the dynamic range of the piece of gear, and the signal's waveform is literally squared, or clipped, off. (see Figure 1)

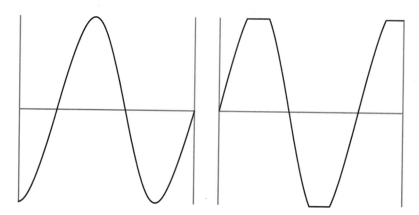

Figure 1 These two waveforms should have similar shapes. The level of the one on the left is low enough to allow it to pass without distortion. The one on the right is too "hot," and has exceeded the dynamic range of a piece of audio gear. It has been "clipped" or distorted. This will result in a raw, buzzy tonality.

Dynamic range can also be applied to acoustic signals. For example, an orchestra is capable of an extremely wide dynamic range, from almost inaudible sounds to very loud bombastic peaks.

In some styles of music, the dynamic range of recordings is often compressed or limited radically. This raises the average level of the music, making it seem louder to the listener.

Phase

The term phase describes the relationship of two waves or signals in time. Each wave is continually passing through its 360-degree cycle of peak and trough (see Figure 2); if two identical waves that are at different points in their cycles are combined, problems can occur.

Figure 2 A sound wave travels in a continuous series of peaks and troughs whose progress is measured in degrees.

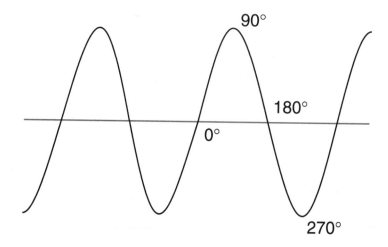

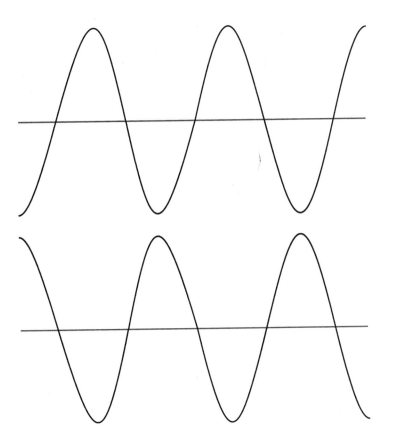

Figure 3 These two wave-forms are 180° out of phase. If they are combined, they will cancel each other out completely resulting in silence. But cancellation can occur if waves are even a little bit out of phase, producing a "hollow" thin sound with reduced volume.

Phase is extremely important in recording, since waves that are out of phase by even a small amount can cancel each other, resulting in tonal changes (see Figure 3). Likewise, waves that are in phase reinforce each other, making the signal stronger. Most commonly, phase problems will occur when using more than one microphone to capture a source; if one mic is further from the source than the other, the resulting signals may be out of phase. One way to prevent this is to use the 3:1 Rule, which states that if two mics are used, the second should be at least three times as far from the source as the first.

Note that many mixers offer "phase" switches (it's more politically correct to call them "polarity" switches), which change the polarity of a signal by 180 degrees.

ones and zeros

A quick tour through the world of digital audio

BY MITCH GALLAGHER

the last few years have been a time of truly wonderful advances at all levels of the music production world. From major, top-of-the-class pro studios to home desktop studios, musicmakers at all levels now have access to many of the same sorts of tools and capabilities. I won't tell you that a desktop studio can necessarily equal all aspects of a mega-dollar commercial facility, but I will say that it's absolutely possible to approach, if not rival, the quality of many professionally realized productions, especially if you know what you're doing with the gear you have. It's likely that some, if not most, of the newer music you've heard on CD, television, radio, and even at the movies was created at least partially at home. And have you checked out the Internet lately? Myriad musicians and hobbyists are creating music at home and making it available for free download, or even for sale, via the Web.

The main reason for the increase in the quality of home-based productions is the advent of affordable digital audio gear. Digital recorders, mixers, and effects are now available that offer previously unheard-of capabilities and audio quality at prices just about anyone can afford.

But the gear is only part of the equation; you have to know what to do with that gear in order to create great-sounding music. This article will zero in on digital audio—the who, what, when, where, why, and how of it, and even more important, the things you need to know to get the most from it. We're going to focus on the essential things you need to know without getting overly tweaky. Remember, the idea isn't to pass a digital electronics certification test, it's to make music!

An Apt Analogy

To better understand where we are, let's take a brief look at where we came from. In the process a few important concepts will come to light, and you'll encounter some of those infamous buzzwords you see thrown around so frequently in audio magazines and advertisements—words like "warmth," "fat," and "saturation."

Until just a few years ago, the predominant method for recording audio, whether at home or in pro studios, was using magnetic tape. The sound waves were converted into electrical voltages using a microphone or pickup, then sent down wires to a tape recorder, where the signal was used to magnetize metal particles on a length of tape. The magnetic patterns on the tape resembled the patterns of the sound waves in the air and the voltages in the wires; they were said to be "analogs" of the original signal—thus the name "analog recording."

All of this worked quite well; countless recordings were, and many still are, recorded using analog methods. Even so-called "all-digital" studios still rely on some analog devices in the creation of music.

But the analog world has some drawbacks, particularly where tape is involved: The frequency response of tape is often limited, making it difficult to capture delicate or complex sounds accurately. The motion of the tape across the recorder's playback and record heads creates noise and hiss. If you need to copy from one tape to another or combine tracks together, you'll add noise and probably lose some treble response. (This is called generation loss.) Tape begins to degrade as soon as signal is recorded on it; the magnetic patterns start to fade, and even worse, may print through from one layer of tape on a reel to another. Good quality analog gear and tape is expensive, and it must be maintained and stored carefully. The only way to edit an analog recording is by using the erase button or by cutting up and reassembling the analog tape using a razor blade and splicing tape—hope you've got a steady hand!

Still, there are some positives to analog recording gear and tape. Analog gear is generally easy to learn and use. Even more important, there's a certain sound to analog recordings that some engineers and musicians prize. Analog tape, in particular, lends a warm, fat quality to the audio recorded on it. This is due to what happens when the tape is saturated with magnetic signals; rather than distorting harshly as digital gear does (as we'll see below), it rounds off and plumps up harsh, sharp edges in a gentle, pleasing manner. Drums and percussive sounds especially can benefit from tape saturation.

Technospeak:
Bits, Bytes, Words, and Samples

Over the past few years, those of us inhabiting the digital audio industry have stolen a number of computer terms and twisted their meanings to fit our own nefarious purposes. Some of those terms could perhaps bear a little explanation: *Bit* is short for BInary digiT. It is, quite simply, either a one or a zero. Bits are gathered into groups of eight called *bytes*. In the computer world, two bytes (16 bits) are gathered together into a *word*. A *sample* (in audio) is a single measurement of amplitude and does not imply a specific bit depth. To make things even more confusing, in the audio industry we have taken over the "word" concept and now use it to describe any single sample, no matter how many bits we use to measure it. Thus you'll hear terms such as "8-bit word" or "20-bit word," which make little sense in computer terms, but quite accurately describe the way bits are grouped in digital audio.

Living in the Digital World

But time and technology march on. The digital revolution has come to the audio world and has solved many of the problems inherent in the analog recording processes of days gone by. Digital has no background noise problems. It's cheap and efficient. There are no generation loss or degradation issues. And maybe coolest of all, digital audio is easy to edit with a computer and the right piece of software.

In the beginning, the big drawback to digital audio (at least among naysayers) was its sound quality. Some felt digital recordings sounded harsh. (Whether some of that harshness might actually have been caused by engineers still applying their old analog recording techniques to the new digital media is a debate we won't get into here.) More significantly, there was no tape saturation to aid in warming or fattening up signals—with digital, what you record is pretty much what you get. And early on, the resolution of digital audio gear was pretty limited, resulting in sonic quality that was often inferior to that provided by good analog gear. These days, though, most musicians and engineers agree that digital audio sounds fine; there are even processes available that can digitally simulate some of the positive effects of recording audio to analog tape.

The Nitty-Gritty

Before we can discuss how to get the most out of digital audio, we need to establish a bit of background knowledge. Don't worry—no need to put on your propeller beanie; we're going to keep this simple and straight-ahead.

Internal versus External Converters

I'm often asked if it's better to have a system's A/D and D/A converters on the soundcard in a computer or mounted in an external box. Ideally, you're better off having the sensitive converter circuits as far from the computer as possible; it's difficult to conceive of a more converter-hostile environment than the inside of a PC! Having said that, in most cases, soundcard manufacturers have done a great job of curtailing potential noise problems caused by the proximity of the card to the computer's guts.

If you do decide to go for a soundcard that has an external converter box, be sure that's really what you're getting. I can think of at least one manufacturer who offered a soundcard/external breakout box combination in which the converters were still mounted on the soundcard in the computer—the breakout box contained only the ¼" connectors. One advantage of a soundcard that has S/PDIF, AES/EBU, or lightpipe digital connections on it is that you're able to use it with whatever external analog-to-digital and digital-to-analog converters you like. The card simply serves as a conduit for getting the digital signal from the converter into the computer. This is one easy (although not always inexpensive) way to upgrade the quality of your studio: Improve the quality of the converters you're using. Manufacturers such as Apogee, Sonorus, SEK'd, Lucid Technology, Frontier Design Group, and others make high-quality external converters that can greatly improve the quality of the raw audio you're capturing.

Remember a few paragraphs ago when we discussed how analog recording systems store a representation of a sound as magnetic patterns? Digital simply modernizes that process. Rather than using magnetism, a circuit called an analog-to-digital converter (a.k.a. A-to-D, A-D, A/D, or ADC) is used to translate the audio into a stream of numbers; zeros and ones, to be precise. (If you're familiar at all with computers, you know that computers speak this same language of zeros and ones; this will be important to remember later on.) All those numbers (referred to as bits) must be stored somewhere: tape, hard drive, compact disc, and MiniDisc are all common digital storage media. When it's time to play the stored digital audio back, a digital-to-analog converter (a.k.a. D-to-A, D-A, D/A, or DAC) changes all those zeros and ones back into sound.

On the surface, that's about all there is to it. But let's dig a little deeper: An analog-to-digital converter works by "sampling" the audio waveform—sort of like taking a ruler and measuring the depth of a puddle of water. But with audio, it's probably more accurate to say that sampling is like using a ruler to measure the depth of the surface of a lake in a strong wind. Under the effects of the wind, the lake surface is constantly changing height as waves blow past. You'd have to measure many times in quick succession to be able to get a real picture of how deep the water is at any given time. Audio is much the same; sound waves are moving through the A/D converter at an incredibly fast rate.

The highest frequency that humans can hear is generally accepted to be around 20,000 Hertz (20kHz). For mathematical reasons it turns out that in order to accurately document an audio waveform, you must sample it twice per cycle, so the minimum sample rate required to capture that 20kHz waveform is 40kHz. Add in a bit of extra room for technical reasons and you have the CD-standard sample rate of 44.1kHz. Some audio gear samples at much higher rates: 48, 88.2, and 96kHz rates are commonplace. Once DVD catches on, expect to see rates up to 192kHz. All other things being equal, a higher sample rate is better (see Figure 1), although as we'll see later there are tradeoffs to using higher sample rates.

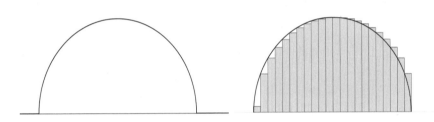

Figure 1 A smooth curve is similar to the way in which analog tape represents an audio waveform. Digital works differently, sampling the curve at various points along its length. Taking more samples (a higher sample rate) and increasing resolution (a higher bit depth) results in a more accurate digital picture of the smooth curve.

The other aspect to sampling is resolution. To go back to our ruler-in-the-water metaphor, if our ruler is divided into inches, we can accurately measure only to the nearest inch. If we subdivide to, say, 1/16-inch markings, the resolution of our measurements can be much more accurate.

With digital audio, the resolution is determined by the number of bits used by the converter to represent the samples. It works like this: Each bit has two possible values, one and zero, so each additional bit doubles the resolution. If we have a two-bit sample, each bit has two possible values, so by using both bits we can represent four possible values. Three bits gives us eight possible values, and so on. When digital audio gear first hit the street, it had a resolution of eight bits, which could provide up to 256 values to represent an audio wave. A 16-bit system provides 65,536 possible values; if we go to 20 bits, we get 1,048,576 values, at 24 bits the number jumps to 16,777,216 possible values (see Figure 2).

In audio terms, each bit of resolution translates into about 6dB of dynamic range (the difference between the softest and the loudest sounds that can be represented). So a 16-bit compact disc has a dynamic range of 96dB; a 20-bit system jumps this to 120dB. A 24-bit system has a theoretical dynamic range of 144dB, although for technical reasons, the current real-world limit is about 120dB, even with a 24-bit converter. It's very important to note that the extra dynamic range a 20- or 24-bit

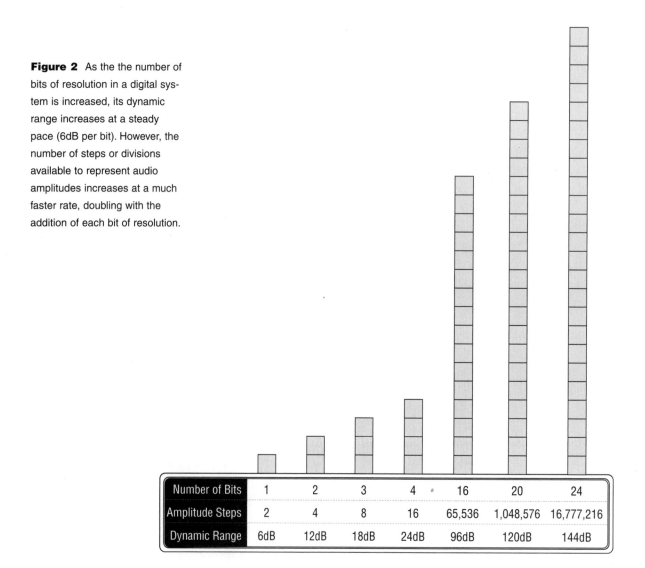

Figure 2 As the the number of bits of resolution in a digital system is increased, its dynamic range increases at a steady pace (6dB per bit). However, the number of steps or divisions available to represent audio amplitudes increases at a much faster rate, doubling with the addition of each bit of resolution.

Number of Bits	1	2	3	4	16	20	24
Amplitude Steps	2	4	8	16	65,536	1,048,576	16,777,216
Dynamic Range	6dB	12dB	18dB	24dB	96dB	120dB	144dB

converter provides isn't on the high (loud) end of the scale. Rather, a 20- or 24-bit converter can more accurately represent quiet sounds—the bottom of the scale is pushed down instead of the top being pushed up (see Figure 3).

The other thing to be aware of is that there is no forgiveness with digital audio! Once you've exceeded the maximum level that a converter can handle, the system will distort. And not in the warm, pleasant way in which analog distorts: Digital overload is a harsh, unpleasant distortion that's best avoided—unless, of course, that's the sound you're after . . . .

It's probably self-evident, but as with sample rates, higher bit depths (the number of bits used to represent a sample) are better, all other things being equal. And as with sample rates, there are tradeoffs to higher bit depths. The primary trade-off is swiftly increasing storage space requirements. A minute of stereo

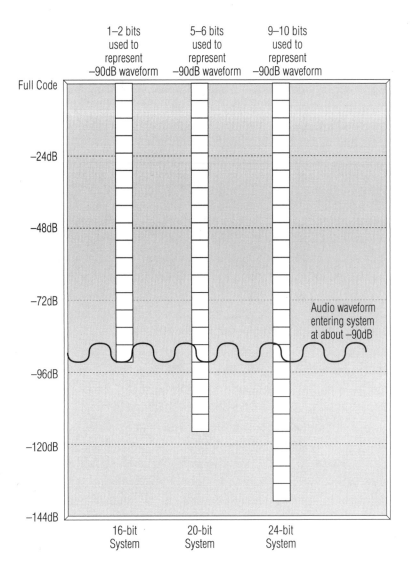

Full Code

1–2 bits used to represent –90dB waveform

5–6 bits used to represent –90dB waveform

9–10 bits used to represent –90dB waveform

–24dB

–48dB

–72dB

Audio waveform entering system at about –90dB

–96dB

–120dB

–144dB

16-bit System

20-bit System

24-bit System

Figure 3 As the bit depth or resolution of a digital system is increased, its ability to represent low-level audio signals is improved. Here we see that in a 16-bit system, the resolution available to represent a low-level signal is minimal. In the 20- and 24-bit systems, there is significantly more resolution available to represent the same wave.

44.1kHz/16-bit audio, such as you'd find on a compact disc, requires around 10MB of storage space. Increasing the bit depth to 24-bit boosts this to over 15MB per minute of stereo audio. If we double the sample rate, we'll need more than 30MB of space for each minute of stereo audio. If you're working on a multitrack session, storage requirements will quickly become quite large: One minute of a 24-track recording with an 88.2kHz/24-bit resolution needs a whopping 360MB of storage space! But it doesn't stop there; your digital system (whether it's a computer or a stand-alone system) has to be powerful enough to shuffle all that data around without stuttering.

In the end, the only way to decide on how much resolution you need is to use your ears. But in my experience, the bit depth of digital audio has far more impact on the sound quality than the sample rate. If you're working with rock, dance,

The Digital Format Jungle

A number of standard formats are used for connecting various pieces of digital gear together; in most cases they're incompatible, so as you plan your system, take into account how you're going to interface things together. Here's a brief rundown on the formats you'll most likely run into:

S/PDIF—Sony/Philips Digital Interface. A common two-channel interconnect standard used on consumer, semi-pro, and some pro digital audio gear. Two interconnect types are used: Coaxial, which normally uses RCA connectors, and optical (sometimes called TOS-link), which uses fiber-optic cables and connections. There are hardware boxes available that can convert a signal from optical S/PDIF to coaxial S/PDIF. Coaxial S/PDIF is an electronically unbalanced protocol, so try to keep your cable runs as short as possible.

AES/EBU—Audio Engineering Society/European Broadcast Union. The "pro" two-channel interconnect standard for digital audio gear. Normally uses 3-pin XLR connectors, but occasionally you'll see it on ¼" jacks. AES/EBU is an electronically balanced protocol, so you can run it for fairly long distances. Interestingly, you can often plug AES and S/PDIF gear together without problems—but there's no guarantee that your data will arrive intact if you mix protocols. It's best to choose one and stick with it.

ADAT Lightpipe—Alesis's ADAT eight-track digital recorder set the audio world on its collective ear when it was first released. Among its innovations was the "lightpipe" standard, an eight-track optical format that has since been adopted by many other manufacturers of digital audio equipment. Lightpipe connectors are found on digital tape decks, computer soundcards, effects processors, and digital mixers. Despite the fact that the connectors look the same as the ones used for optical S/PDIF, the two formats are not compatible.

TDIF—TASCAM's DA-88 eight-track digital recorder introduced another digital format to the fray. The eight-channel TDIF standard uses multi-pin connectors and wire cables rather than optical connections. You'll find TDIF supported by digital tape decks, computer soundcards, and digital mixers. It is possible to convert between lightpipe and TDIF using special hardware boxes, but it's often easier to choose one format and stick to it throughout your studio.

In most cases, interfacing pieces of digital gear together is an easy process; aside from plugging the cables in correctly (outputs go to inputs) the only other issue is making sure that the various items are clocked together. (Clock information is used to ensure that the sample rates of the various devices are synchronized.) This involves setting devices that will be receiving digital information to look for external sync. All of the protocols listed above carry clock sync embedded in their signals, so there's no usually need to run separate clock connections between devices.

techno, or pop styles, it's questionable whether you'll hear much difference with higher sample rates or bit depths; if you work with delicate acoustic material, then the effects of higher resolutions may be audible to you. Keep in mind that, for now at least, the primary resolution for delivering music to listeners is 44.1kHz/16-bit (often referred to as "CD-quality"). This may change as the DVD format becomes more available and popular.

Eight Things to Remember
When Working with Digital Audio

- Keep audio levels as high as possible short of clipping. Digital audio systems provide the best resolution when you're maxing them out—distortion increases substantially at very low levels (the opposite of analog systems). That said, digital distortion sounds pretty ugly. Leave yourself enough headroom to prevent clipping.

- Of digital bondage: The master/slave relationship. If you're connecting two pieces of audio gear together digitally, one of them must be the master, the other the slave. Usually the source of the digital signal will be the master, while the device that's receiving that signal will be the slave. For example, if you're transferring audio from an Alesis ADAT digital tape machine into a computer using a digital connection, the computer should be set to sync to external digital clock so that it slaves its sample rate to the ADAT. If you're transferring from the computer to the ADAT, the master/slave relationship should be reversed.

- Keep sample rates and bit depths matched when transferring between digital devices. Sending a 24-bit signal into a 16-bit device will result in eight bits of resolution being lost. Playing a track back at the wrong sample rate will result in it being either sharp or flat compared to other tracks. If possible, keep the bit depth and sample rate consistent throughout your studio and among your various projects.

- Avoid unnecessary analog-to-digital and digital-to-analog conversions. Once a signal is in the digital domain, try to keep it there. Extra conversions can result in degradation to the signal. If you use an external digital reverb hooked up with analog connections, for example, the reverb will be internally converting from analog to digital and back, adding two extra conversion stages.

One ideal example would be to record your audio into a computer. Do all your processing internally using plug-ins, then burn a CD directly from the computer files. In this case, once the audio is in the computer, it doesn't get converted back to analog until the listener plays it in his or her CD player.

- Listen for tiny clicks and pops during transfers. Clicks and pops during digital audio transfers usually mean that there's a clock problem somewhere in your system. Verify that your connections are correct, then make sure that the master/slave relationship between the gear is set up properly.

- Stay high-resolution for as long as possible. If you're working with high-resolution digital audio (greater than 16-bit/44.1kHz resolution), don't reduce the resolution until the last possible moment. Usually the time to convert is as you master a recording for burning to CD.

- Digital meters work differently from analog meters. With analog, when your levels hit "0" you've normally got quite a bit of room left before the system distorts. With digital, "0" is it—go past it and you're in distortion-land. For this reason, a signal that reads out at 0VU on an analog system will generally show up as –12 or –18dB on a digital meter. This is perfectly normal—the meters just reference the levels differently.

- Back up! In general, digital is much hardier stuff than analog, but things can go wrong with it: Storage media can fail. Digital tapes can have dropouts or get eaten by tape machines. Hard drives can crash. Be sure to back up anything you'd regret losing. CD-R makes a great backup medium, but use whatever appeals to you (see "Data Backup" on page 162 for more on backing up to CD-R and CD-RW).

No More Razor Blades

As mentioned earlier, the only way to edit analog recordings was with a razor blade. The engineer would find the edit locations by manually rocking the reel of tape back and forth until he or she could hear the spot where the edit needed to be made. After marking that spot with a white grease pencil, the engineer would pull the tape off the reel and physically cut it apart with a razor blade. Once all the cuts were made, the various pieces of tape would be stuck back together (hopefully in the right order) using special splicing tape. Not much fun, and not for the faint of heart, either! Picture an engineer taking a razor blade to a one-of-a-kind master multitrack recording made by a platinum-selling band—just a little pressure!

Thankfully, the digital revolution has changed all that. Digital audio is stored as the same type of data that computers like to chew on, so it was no great leap to put PCs, Macs, and stand-alone hard disk recorders to work as audio editors. The advantages to using digital audio systems for editing audio are many: It's far more precise than using a razor blade (to say nothing of the reduction in bloody fingers). You can undo most operations if you make a mistake (this is called non-destructive editing). Since you can view the digital audio visually on the computer or LCD screen, it's very easy to locate the point you want to work on. You can easily create multiple versions of a file to try out different edits. The list goes on.

One other advantage is that computers use hard disks to store digital audio (as do many stand-alone digital recorders/mixers such as Roland's VS-880, Akai's DPS-12, and Korg's D16). Hard drives by nature are random access devices; they can instantly (well, almost instantly) jump their read heads to any location on the disk and read the information there. There's no need to wait for a tape machine to fast-forward or rewind to the correct spot.

Of course, computers and stand-alone hard disk/MiniDisc recorders/mixers offer many other benefits; a big one is DSP capabilities. DSP (digital signal processing) is the application of specialized algorithms, such as equalization, normalizing, noise reduction, and so on, to audio files. DSP also encompasses the world of effects such as reverb, delay, chorus, and distortion. In addition, DSP can be used to model or emulate the way a particular piece of gear works. For example, there are DSP-based processes that attempt to exactly duplicate the sound of vintage guitar amplifiers, audio compressors, and even microphones. As processing chips get more and more powerful, expect to see most, if not all, processing of audio being done using DSP.

Just a Bit More ...

These days it's almost possible to create an entirely digital studio; about the only things that absolutely have to be analog are microphones and speakers. (There are so-called "digital" speakers and mics currently on the market, but these are actually conventional analog units that contain built-in D/A or A/D converters. While there are some advantages to this approach, it doesn't make them true digital items.) Most people view this move toward the digital world as a positive, although a few stalwarts cling to the analog past with amazing fervor.

For the rest of us, the shift to digital has been a beautiful thing. The gear we have today provides amazing power and sound quality for an ever-dropping entry price, and the future promises even more powerful gear for an even lower price. What more could you ask for?

making music with MIDI

BY JIM AIKIN

I f you're inclined to use the words "music" and "computer" in the same sentence, then sooner or later (and probably sooner) you're going to find yourself using MIDI. In the next few pages you'll learn everything you need to know in order to make music with MIDI. Not everything there is to know about MIDI—that would take a few more pages, and would involve some fairly technical discussions—but enough to get you off to a flying start.

Along the way we'll touch on a number of details that you may not need to know...for a while, until one day you need to know something specific, and you're digging through your stack of old magazines, muttering, "Now where did that copy of *Music & Computers* get to?" I promise not to use the word "byte," but even so, the discussion may get a wee bit technical here and there. If this scares you, take a deep breath and remember: Anything that's truly worth doing is worth putting a little effort into.

What Is MIDI?

MIDI is a way of sending music performance information from one place to another. The letters are an abbreviation for Musical Instrument Digital Interface, and they're pronounced "middy," not "my-die."

MIDI can be used entirely within a computer—for example, when one music software program sends MIDI messages to another program, or to a soundcard. More often, though, MIDI messages travel down MIDI cables from one hardware device (such as a computer) to another (such as a synthesizer). A MIDI cable carries information in only one direction, so if you want the computer and synthesizer to be able to talk to one another, you need two cables—one from the computer's MIDI out to the synth's MIDI in, and the other from the synth's MIDI out back to the computer's MIDI in. This basic hookup is illustrated in Figure 1.

Let's go back to the phrase "music performance information." What does that mean? It means that a stream of MIDI messages contains some fairly exact infor-

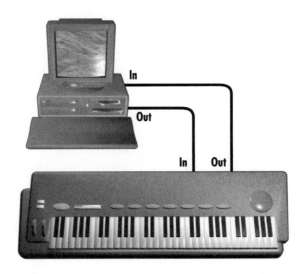

Figure 1 A simple computer-based MIDI system. The keyboard's MIDI out is connected to the computer's MIDI in, and vice-versa. With this system you can record your keyboard performances into the computer, edit them, and play them back. You can also use the keyboard to play either the synth chip on your sound-card or a software-based synthesizer.

mation, in a form the computer can understand, about a musical performance. Not just any performance, though: The music has to be played on some type of MIDI-compatible musical instrument. That usually means a keyboard, though other types of MIDI performance instruments, such as MIDI guitars and MIDI wind instruments, are available. The device that generates the MIDI signals is often called a controller, because its output is used to control some other device. If it's a keyboard, it may be referred to as a master keyboard.

Here's how MIDI performance information works: Let's say I'm playing a MIDI master keyboard. Each time I strike a key, a new MIDI message is generated. This message contains the essential information about what I just did: which key I've played, and how hard I hit it. The idea is illustrated in Figure 2. When I lift my finger, another MIDI message is generated. The first message starts a note, so it's called, logically enough, a note-on message. The second message stops the note, so it's called a note-off message. Pretty simple, when you think about it.

Figure 2 Striking a key on a MIDI keyboard sends a MIDI note-on message (left). Lifting your finger from the key sends a MIDI note-off message (right). These messages can be stored and edited in a computer sequencer program.

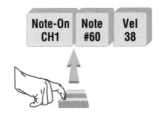

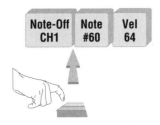

What Is MIDI Used For?

In your explorations of computer-based music, you'll find that you're using MIDI in some (or all) of the following ways:

- To record a performance on a MIDI keyboard into a computer using sequencer software, and then play it back.
- To build up complete musical arrangements (melody, chords, bass, drums, and so on) using sequencer software, edit the arrangements in the computer, and perhaps print them out as sheet music.

- To download MIDI songs from the Internet and play them back using your computer's soundcard or a software synthesizer as a MIDI sound source.
- To play a MIDI sound source (some type of tabletop or rackmount tone module) directly from a MIDI keyboard, with or without the aid of a computer.
- To synchronize the timing of two or more music playback devices, such as software-based recorders.
- To use a computer for long-term storage of the data in the memory banks of a hardware synthesizer.

If I were playing a non-MIDI instrument—say, a clarinet—you could put a microphone up in front of me and capture my musical performance as an audio recording (either on tape, or in a computer equipped with an audio input and audio recording software). In some sense, the audio recording would contain "performance information." But in fact, the recording would contain only the actual sound of my performance; it would contain no information about which fingers I had pressed down on which clarinet keys. You'd have to be a trained clarinet player to figure that out by listening to the recording. If I were playing a guitar, the recording would contain no information about which string I plucked to create a specific note, only the actual sound of the note.

MIDI is just the opposite: It contains no information about the actual sound. But it contains some precise details about what the performer's fingers did, and when. Sending a MIDI note-on message is a bit like sending a telegram to a soprano instructing her to sing Middle C. She could be hoarse, in fine voice, enthusiastic but entirely untrained, or even tone-deaf. The telegram would be exactly the same in any case, even though the sound itself would be radically different. This is what we mean when we say, "MIDI isn't audio."

MIDI is a realtime communications protocol. This means that when a MIDI message is received by a MIDI device, the receiving device responds to the message immediately. This fact is crucial: If you're using a MIDI controller keyboard to play a remote sound-generating device (such as a synthesizer or sampler located in a rack across the room), you don't want to hear the sound three seconds later. Even a tenth of a second is too much time lag. MIDI is just barely fast enough to deal with music performance without perceptible time lags.

How fast is "just barely fast enough"? That's one of those technical areas we don't have room to get into. Suffice it to say that it takes about 1ms (one millisecond, or a thousandth of a second) to transmit one MIDI note-on message. Once in a while you may get into a musical situation where the MIDI messages are flying so thick and fast that they get backed up, in which case the timing of the music may start to get noticeably sloppy or uneven, but that's relatively rare, and not something you need to worry about.

Setting Up Your MIDI Equipment

If you're using a Windows computer with a soundcard and multimedia-type speakers, you probably already have all the equipment you need to get started making music with MIDI. As you get into it, you'll undoubtedly want more equipment: There are a lot of things that a computer by itself just can't do. Let's build up a decent MIDI equipment setup one item at a time. As we go along, we'll see how they all fit together.

The first thing you need is a software program called a sequencer. A sequencer is used for recording, editing, and playing back MIDI data, and MIDI songs are often called sequences. A decent MIDI sequencer can be had for as little as $29, or you can spend almost a thousand dollars on a pro-level program. (For more on sequencers, see "Software for the Studio" on page 65.) In some sense, the sequencer is the brains of a MIDI setup. It's used not only for playing back MIDI data but for routing MIDI messages from one place in your system to another.

Your soundcard probably already has a synthesizer on it, in the form of a special synth chip. This chip is a MIDI device, just like a MIDI keyboard or tone module. After downloading a MIDI sequence from the Internet (in a file format called a Standard MIDI File, or SMF), you can load the file into your sequencer, direct the sequencer's data output to the synth chip, and listen to the music through the multimedia speakers. If you like, you can use the sequencer's editing commands to put the music in a different key, add verses, change the drum part, or whatever you like. This can all be done using a mouse and convenient graphic-based tools within the sequencer—no additional hardware is required.

The next step is to add a MIDI keyboard. If your soundcard has a joystick port, you'll probably be able to add a simple MIDI connector to it, which will allow you to hook the keyboard to the computer. This hookup is shown in Figure 1. If you're using a Macintosh, or if your PC soundcard isn't MIDI-equipped, you may need to add a separate piece of hardware called a MIDI interface. This interface allows you to get MIDI messages into and out of the computer. We'll have more to say below about MIDI interfaces.

If your keyboard has built-in speakers, you're set. Otherwise, you'll need some way to listen to it. Remember, MIDI is not audio. Because of this, hooking up the MIDI cables as shown in Figure 1 will not send the keyboard's audio (sound) output to the multimedia speakers. You may be able to accomplish this by hooking the keyboard's audio out to the soundcard's line in jack, but I wouldn't recommend it, as the keyboard's output could easily blow out your speakers. A better idea is to invest in a small audio mixer and a pair of powered monitor speakers.

When you first hook your keyboard to your computer, you'll quickly discover that you need to know a little about how MIDI signals are routed from place to place. You may find that the keyboard sounds a little strange—sort of tinny or hollow—when it's MIDIed up to the computer. Or you might suddenly hear some other sound layered with the one you selected—a banjo plunking along with each note that comes from the string orchestra, for example. You may also find that suddenly your keyboard will play only half as many notes at once as it could play before (though with modern keyboards, most of which can play 64 notes at once, you may never notice that you're suddenly reduced to 32 notes unless you have a lot of fingers).

These problems are easily solved. In order to understand them, we need to trace the MIDI signal flow. For reference, take a look at Figure 3. When you press a key on the keyboard, the keyboard (that is, the row of black-and-white things itself, not the instrument as a whole with its buttons and so on) sends out a note-

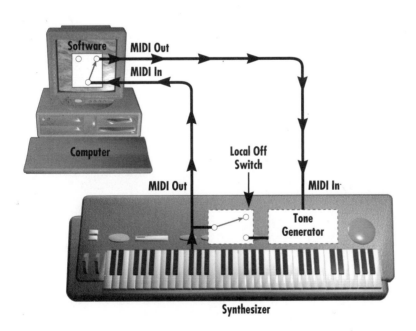

Figure 3   The computer sequencer (top) has a feature called "software thru" or "MIDI echo." This feature, which can be switched on or off, causes MIDI messages that appear at the sequencer's MIDI input to be passed immediately back to the output. While useful, this feature can cause problems if you don't understand what it's doing. The music keyboard (bottom) is equipped with a setting called "Local On/Off." This setting controls whether the keys on the keyboard send MIDI messages to the instrument's internal tone generator, or only to the MIDI out jack. If both software thru and local on are switched on, each time you play a key the MIDI note message will reach the tone generator twice. To prevent this problem, either switch the keyboard to local off, or switch off the sequencer's software thru.

on message. This message travels to the circuit board inside the instrument (called a tone generator) that actually makes the sound. The tone generator obligingly starts playing a note.

At the same time, the note-on message appears at the keyboard instrument's MIDI out jack and travels down the MIDI cable to the computer. Here it's received by the MIDI sequencer software. If the software is in record mode, the note-on will be recorded as the start of a new note, for later playback and/or editing. But in any case, the sequencer will probably turn around and immediately send the note-on back to the computer's MIDI out jack. This feature is called the sequencer's software thru or MIDI echo. The note-on runs back down the other MIDI cable and shortly reaches the keyboard's MIDI in jack. From here, it's routed to the keyboard's tone generator, which responds by starting to play a note.

Do you see the problem? The same note-on message has reached the keyboard instrument's tone generator twice—first coming directly from the keyboard itself, and then again coming back from the computer. Two notes are now playing, which is probably not what you'll expect or want when you're playing only one key.

There are two places where you can intercept the note-on message. You can switch off the sequencer's software thru. Or you can switch the keyboard instrument into a mode called local-off mode. In local-off mode, the keyboard on a MIDI instrument sends messages out of the MIDI out jack, but it doesn't send them to its own tone generator. The tone generator responds only to MIDI messages arriving at the instrument's MIDI in jack. With a bigger MIDI equipment rig, method two is preferable to method one, for reasons we won't try to nail down here.

A more sophisticated MIDI/computer setup is shown in Figure 4. Rather than rely on one keyboard to produce the sound of an entire musical arrangement, we're adding a tone module of some sort (either a synthesizer or a sampler). At this point, the keyboard might be playing the bass and string orchestra chord sounds, while the module plays the drums and the melody.

In fact, each might be playing six or eight different kinds of sounds at once. For this to work, each unit must be set to multitimbral mode (often called simply "multi" or "combi" mode). If this sounds complicated or mystical, it's because we haven't yet tackled the subject of MIDI channels. So let's get started.

MIDI Messages: The Nuts and Bolts

So far, we've mentioned only two closely related types of MIDI messages—the note-on and note-off messages. A number of types of messages are defined for MIDI communications. Some of these have clearly defined meanings—they're used strictly for one type of musical task, and any device that's configured to respond to them is supposed to do so in a predictable way. Others are defined a little more loosely. Send one of the latter to a MIDI synth, and it might do almost anything. Or it might do nothing. It's pretty much up to the receiving device to decide how or whether to respond to a given MIDI message. Because a MIDI cable carries messages in only one direction, the device that sends the message normally has no information about what's happening at the receiving end. The receiver could be switched off, or could be malfunctioning in some horrible way, and the sender will never know.

Channels.   At the highest level, MIDI defines two types of messages: system messages and channel messages. System messages are kind of a grab-bag, and we won't have much to say about them in this chapter. The messages used for actually playing music are the channel messages.

MIDI defines 16 channels. This means that a channel-type message, such as a note-on or note-off, is always on one channel or another; for example, we can talk about a note-on on channel 3. Messages on all 16 channels can be flying down the same MIDI cable at more or less the same time, all mixed together with one another. The situation is similar to what happens in the cable hooked up to your TV. All of the channel information for NBC, Fox, MTV, CNN, and so on is flying down the same cable at the same time. Your TV set will normally receive the information arriving on one particular channel, and ignore all the other channels.

In exactly the same way, a MIDI synthesizer set to receive on channel 1 will simply ignore channel messages on the other 15 channels. But modern synths are a little more versatile than that. Most can be set up so as to respond on several channels at the same time. Each channel is normally dedicated to making a single type of sound. So one synthesizer could be playing the bass sound on channel 1, the string orchestra on channel 2, the melody on channel 3, and the drums on channel 10, all at the same time. It's a little like having one TV set with four screens, or even more.

It's important to understand, however, that each type of synthesizer has a strict upper limit on how many notes it can play at once. That limit might be only eight notes, or 16, or 64, or some other number. If it will play only 12 notes at a time, when you send it note-ons on all 16 channels at once, some of the notes won't get played. That's one of the reasons why you may want a setup with more than one tone generator, like the one shown in Figure 4. If the keyboard in Figure 4 is set to respond on channels 1 through 4, and the module is set to respond on channels 5 through 8, you (or, to be more practical, your computer) can play arrangements with eight independent musical parts all pumping at once, with much less danger of running out of notes.

Figure 4 When we add a MIDI tone module to the setup shown in Figure 1, we need to pay closer attention to the MIDI signal flow. Note that the module is connected to the keyboard's MIDI thru jack. A MIDI thru jack passes on whatever messages are received at the MIDI in jack — but messages that are sent out of the keyboard's MIDI out are not sent out of the thru. As a result, when we want to play the module from the keyboard, the computer has to be switched on. Messages from the keyboard pass through the computer and return to the keyboard, as in Figure 1, but now they flow onward from the keyboard to the module via the thru jack. The keyboard and module are set to respond on different MIDI channels, so the computer can send MIDI to each of them individually.

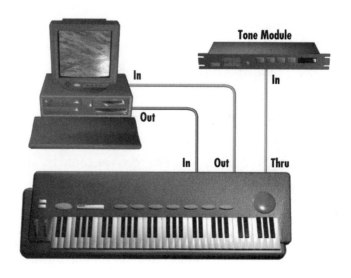

Note-Ons and Note-Offs.   A note-on message contains three essential pieces of information. First, the channel. Second, the note number. Third, the key velocity. Let's take a closer look at each of these.

The *MIDI channel* designation (a number between 1 and 16) we've already discussed. The *note number* will have a value between 0 and 127. On a MIDI keyboard, Middle C is note 60. A standard five-octave keyboard, the type found on many MIDI synths, has 61 keys in a range from note 36 (low C) to note 96 (high C), as shown in Figure 5.

Key velocity is a measurement of how fast the key was traveling between the time when your finger first started to depress it and when it arrived on the keybed (the physical support that runs beneath the keyboard). In other words, the velocity infor-

Figure 5 A typical five-octave MIDI keyboard, showing the note numbers.

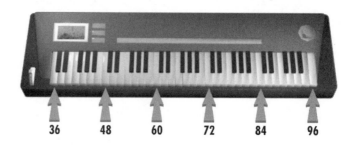

mation corresponds to how hard you struck the key. Velocity values range from 1 to 127. It's important to understand that the velocity value is read only at the time when you strike the key. Pressing down on the key after it has reached the keybed can create a different message called aftertouch (see below), but pressing down won't change the velocity, because the note-on has already been sent.

Velocity is most often used to make the notes sound louder or softer, just as they would on a piano: Strike the key hard and you get a loud, bright sound. Velocity can also be used to control other aspects of the sound; you'll need to consult your synthesizer's manual to learn about the possibilities.

Note-off messages have the same three pieces of information as note-ons, though note-off velocity is usually ignored. It may seem obvious, but for a note-off message to stop the sound of a note that is currently being played, the note number of the note-off has to match the note number of an earlier note-on message that started the note sounding. If the note numbers don't match, the note will never stop playing. The same problem arises if the MIDI cable is unplugged after the note-on is received, but before the note-off is received. Either way, you get the dreaded stuck note.

There are several ways to stop stuck notes, including the most desperate but most effective measure: Switch the offending synthesizer off and back on again. Your sequencer may have a panic button that you can click on with the mouse. This button will send a special MIDI message called an all-notes-off message, which is supposed to shut off any currently sounding notes. Don't worry, though: Stuck notes are quite rare.

For technical reasons, a note-on message with a velocity value of 0 does the same thing as a note-off: It doesn't start a note, it stops a note. This information is not extremely useful, but you might need to know it sometime, so here it is. It explains why other types of MIDI data, such as controllers, can have values from 0 to 127, while note-on velocity can have only the values from 1 to 127.

Aftertouch and Pitchbend. While a note is playing, you may want to make various kinds of changes in its sound: You might want to change the pitch, or add vibrato, for example. MIDI offers numerous ways to do this type of thing.

Pitchbend messages are normally generated by a hardware controller of some sort at the left end of the keyboard—a wheel, lever, joystick, or ribbon (see Figure 6). Pitchbend messages are used to bend the pitch of the note(s) up or down in a smooth, continuous way, generating the kind of expressive lick that a guitarist can make by bending a string sideways. A single pitchbend message tells how far the bender has been moved away from center. Pushing or wiggling a hardware pitchbender

Figure 6 Various types of MIDI controller messages can be generated by the left-hand controller section of a typical keyboard. One of these wheels or levers will usually send pitch-bend messages, while another sends modulation (continuous controller 1), which is often used to add vibrato. Other hard-ware controller devices, if pres-ent, may be designed so as to allow the user to choose which type of MIDI data they will send. Here we're looking at the left-hand controller section of a Korg Z1 synth, which has the expected wheels and also a two-dimensional pad controller. By touching the pad and then moving your fingertip, you can send two different types of con-troller messages at once.

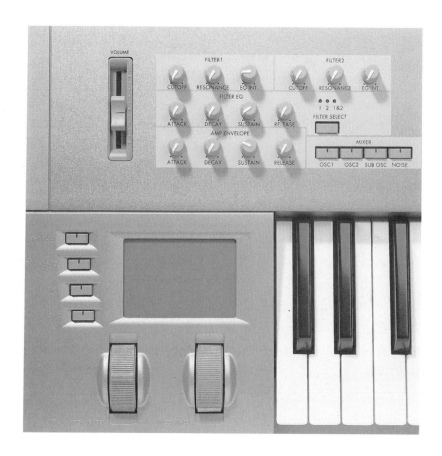

generates a stream of dozens, if not hundreds, of separate pitchbend messages, each corresponding to one momentary position of the bender.

An aftertouch sensor is built into many (though by no means all) keyboards. *After-touch* is generated by pressing down harder on a key after it has reached the keybed. Aftertouch is often used to add vibrato, or to open up the filter so that a note gets brighter in an expressive way (a so-called "wah-wah" effect). But as with many of the continuous controller messages (see below), the musical effect of aftertouch is not defined by the MIDI Specification. Aftertouch messages could add vibrato, or deepen the reverb (a cavernous echo effect), or just about anything else you can imagine, and some things you probably can't. A MIDI synth or tone module receiving aftertouch messages doesn't have to respond to them in any way and the nature of the response depends entirely on the receiving synth, not on the aftertouch message itself. The aftertouch message just says, in essence, "Aftertouch on channel 4, value 36."

This is true even of pitchbend. Though it's almost always used to bend the pitch, it can cause other types of changes in the sound instead of or in addition to bending the pitch, depending on how the receiving synth is programmed. What's more, the receiving synth gets to decide for itself how much pitch change it wants to make in response to a given pitchbend message. If the bend depth parameter in the synth is

Figure 7 The hardware devices shown in Figure 6 generate MIDI data, which appears in the graphic controller edit window of the computer sequencer (in this case Steinberg Cubase) looking like the mountain shape in the lower half of this window. Each stairstep in the contour represents a new controller message. Here we're looking at data for modulation (CC1).

set to an octave, a full-on pitchbend message (the one that's sent when the hardware bender has been pushed as far as possible) will bend the pitch upward by an octave. But if the bend depth is set to a half-step, an identical pitchbend message will cause only a half-step of change. The MIDI message is exactly the same in either case.

There's also a way to change the pitchbend depth of a synth by sending it a MIDI message. But this is an example of using MIDI for remote control. It isn't a pitchbend message at all but a different and more complex type of message that we won't cover here.

Continuous Controllers. MIDI defines a set of 128 different *continuous controller* messages (often called "CCs"). These controllers are numbered from 0 through 127, and each of them can have a data value between 0 and 127. In other words, it makes sense to talk about a controller 1 message on channel 9 with a value of 56.

Some of the controllers have names, and are normally used for specific musical purposes. Controller 1, for example, is the modulation wheel (see Figures 6 and 7). A controller 1 message with a value of 0 is sent when the wheel is pulled all the way back toward the player, and a controller 1 message with a value of 127 is sent when the wheel is pushed all the way forward. Controller 7, which is called Master Volume, is used to control the overall volume of the sound being made on a particular channel. Controller 64 is the sustain pedal.

Other controllers are undefined. And for that matter, what is "modulation wheel"? What does it sound like? It sounds like whatever the receiving synth wants it to sound like. The mod wheel controller is often used to add vibrato, but it might do almost anything.

The term "continuous" is more than a bit misleading, as Figure 7 shows. Each MIDI channel message is a discrete packet containing two or three bytes (oh, darn, I promised I wouldn't use that word...well, just think of them as numbers) traveling down the MIDI cable. If we send a CC1 message on channel 1 with a value of 1, and then five minutes later we send a CC1 message on channel 1 with a value of 2, there's nothing continuous about it. Any number of other MIDI messages could have come between the two. The term "continuous" really means that CCs are usually generated by hardware devices like wheels and joysticks, which can be moved in a continuous fashion.

Also worth noting: In many types of music software and hardware, aftertouch and pitchbend are lumped together in a menu with the continuous controllers. They're used for many of the same kinds of musical effects; the differences are mainly technical.

Program changes. We've talked a bit about how a synth can be set up to play a string-orchestra type sound, a bass sound, a drum sound, and so on. In the instrument, these are called sound programs. (The terms "patches" and "presets" are also commonly used.) Sound programs or just "programs" for short can be selected under remote control using MIDI messages. To do this, you send the synth a program change message.

The original MIDI Specification was adopted in 1983. In those days most synths had 32 programs, or maybe 40. To the people who created MIDI, 128 possible program changes seemed like plenty. In recent years, as synths with hundreds of programs have become common, some way had to be found to call up any of them using MIDI. The solution is a second message called bank select. A bank select message is sent first, telling the synth to switch to a certain bank of programs, and then a program change message selects one of the programs within that bank. Unfortunately, different synths number their banks in different ways. Bank select numbering is one of the screwier areas in MIDI; the way to deal with it is to try different bank select messages until you find the one that calls up the sound you want to hear.

MIDI synchronization. One of the MIDI system messages is called *MIDI clock*. Clock messages are sent by tempo-based MIDI devices such as sequencers and arpeggiators. Twenty-four MIDI clock messages are sent for every quarter-note. A tempo-based receiving device, such as another sequencer or arpeggiator, can respond to the clock messages by speeding up or slowing down if necessary in order to stay in time with the transmitting device. The transmitting device is called the master, and the receiving device is usually called the slave. MIDI clock is a little like a conductor waving a baton. And just as the musicians in the orchestra have to be looking at the conductor if they want to follow the baton, the device that you want to be slaved to a master timing source using MIDI clock must be set to external clock mode. When a device is in internal clock mode, it will ignore the conductor—that is, the MIDI clock messages. There's a lot more to MIDI synchronization than this, but this is enough to get you started.

System-exclusive. System-exclusive (sys-ex) data is a way of sending messages that will be meaningful only to specific devices within a MIDI system. Each manufacturer gets to design their own sys-ex messages, which can do anything the manufacturer feels would be useful. When a sys-ex message is aimed at one synth in a system (such as a Roland JV-80, for example), every other device in the MIDI system will simply ignore it. The exception to this rule is that certain types of computer software are designed to handle sys-ex data of many different types.

Sys-ex is used in a number of ways. Here are the three most common usages:

- The entire memory contents of a synthesizer can be transmitted down a MIDI cable using sys-ex, and stored in a computer. A program called a librarian or editor/librarian is most often used for this, but some sequencers can also record and store sys-ex. This type of message is very large (which is why it's sometimes called a bulk dump), and will entirely tie up a MIDI system for a time ranging from a few seconds to a couple of minutes.

- Some newer synths can load an updated operating system using sys-ex. To take advantage of this feature, you usually have to log onto the manufacturer's Web site, download the sys-ex file, store it on your computer's hard drive, and then play it through your sequencer software so that it's received by the synth for which it's intended. A new operating system can include bug-fixes or entirely new features.

- Some synths transmit short sys-ex messages when you edit their voice parameters from their front panel. For example, if you change the release time of an envelope generator, a string of sys-ex messages may be generated, a new one each time the value of the release time parameter is changed. By recording these messages in a sequencer, you can automate complex sound changes, even in a synth that doesn't allow such changes to be made using continuous controller messages. (Continuous controller messages are a better choice if they're available, as they don't clutter up the MIDI data stream so badly and are easier to edit in the sequencer.)

Troubleshooting Your MIDI Setup

It's happened to us all at one time or another: You turn on your computer, fire up your MIDI keyboard, load a song file, hit the play button — and you don't hear a thing. Here are some common trouble spots, and a few tips on how to fix things.

- Channel mismatch. Is the MIDI transmitter (a sequencer track, for instance) transmitting on one channel, while the receiver is "listening" to a different channel? If so, no sound will be produced.

- Cable routing. Check the entire MIDI signal path, making sure each out or thru jack is hooked up to the in jack on the receiving unit.

- Port configuration error. Your sequencer may be sending MIDI messages off into limbo. Check its "MIDI Setup" menu item to make sure that your interface's driver is selected as the output port.

- Audio problems. Is the volume turned up on the receiving synth? Is its audio output hooked up to your mixer or sound system? Is the mixer switched on? Is the amp switched on?

- Is the track volume turned up? A sequencer's track volume parameter transmits MIDI controller 7, which is normally assigned to control the main volume on a synth. If a very low CC7 value has been sent, the synth won't be heard.

- Was a bank select message sent to the synth that caused it to switch to a bank where there are no sounds stored? In this situation, a synth is supposed to ignore the bank select command, but it might mistakenly try to respond to it.

MIDI Interfaces for Your Computer

You'll need some form of hardware to get MIDI signals in and out of your computer. What hardware you choose depends first on what type of computer you have and second on how large your MIDI setup is. Along with the hardware, you'll need a matching piece of software: a MIDI driver (on the PC) or system extension (on the Macintosh).

With a small equipment rig, your computer will possibly need only one MIDI in jack and one MIDI out jack. (Remember, one MIDI cable can carry music information on 16 channels, which could mean as many as 16 separate synthesizers!) On the PC, this type of MIDI interfacing is often handled by the built-in soundcard. You may have to buy a hardware attachment to hook to the soundcard's joystick port, but the MIDI driver software should be installed automatically when the soundcard is installed at the factory, or when you install its other software after you purchase it. PC MIDI interfaces are also available that hook to serial, parallel, and USB ports.

On the Mac, a MIDI interface will connect either to the printer or modem serial port (on older Macs) or to the USB port (on the new machines). Even a small MIDI interface on the Mac, or a serial or parallel interface on the PC, will usually have two output jacks. Most often these can be separately addressed by the driver/extension software, giving you 32 MIDI channels.

Figure 8   The MIDI Time Piece AV from Mark of the Unicorn. This multiport MIDI interface hooks to a computer and gives you 128 independent channels of input and output.

As your MIDI setup grows, you may find that you need a multiport interface. These devices typically have at least four MIDI ins and eight MIDI outs. They may have other features, too—special jacks for sending and receiving synchronization signals, or the ability to route and process MIDI signals even when the interface isn't hooked to a computer. A typical multiport interface, the Mark of the Unicorn MIDI Time Piece AV, is shown in Figure 8.

Rather than use a dedicated piece of interface hardware, you may want to invest in a synthesizer (either a keyboard or a tone module) that has its own built-in computer interface. Synths with computer interfaces are common in the price range that appeals to home hobbyists, and they work very well, especially in desktop music setups where space is at a premium. Such a synth will usually come with a floppy disk containing the driver/extension software you need. By hooking a special cable between the synth and the computer and then attaching a MIDI cable to the synth's MIDI out jack, you can control other MIDI devices directly from the computer, as well as using the computer to play the sounds within the module or keyboard itself.

MIDI Mastery

I've been using MIDI and computer sequencers for more years than I care to think about. The musical power of these tools never ceases to amaze me. MIDI is really pretty darn simple, considering all you can do with it. I won't say, "The only limit is your imagination," both because that's a terrible cliché and because it isn't true at all. There are many limitations within MIDI, and more limitations reside in the music hardware and software that communicates via MIDI. As powerful as the technology is, it's not magic.

I will say, though, that after all these years I haven't yet come close to reaching the limits of what MIDI and a few good synthesizers can do. And I don't expect I ever will.

putting your studio together

guide to studio equipment

BY MITCH GALLAGHER

putting a studio together can be a lot of fun. Most of us are gear junkies on one level or another—nothing gets our pulse racing like a shiny new piece of hardware or the magic moment when a new software program boots for the first time. Unfortunately, few of us have the resources to spend as much as we want on our rigs. The real world intrudes, and a budget is imposed.

When the word "budget" is used to describe a product, there's often a negative spin. People see the word and assume the product is poorly built and doesn't do much, or doesn't do it very well. But with the current crop of electronic music production gear, the B-word is no longer something to run from. Today's budget gear is of very high quality—often comparable to the so-called "pro" gear of years past. This is good news for those of us who don't have unlimited funds to throw at our music gear obsession. It means that with some careful shopping, we can put together a studio capable of producing great-sounding music and still afford life's necessities; cable television, for example.

On the following pages, you'll find discussions of the various categories of components that go into making up a studio. We'll look at what each is, why you need it, tips on what to look for as you're shopping, and notes on what you're giving up (if anything) by purchasing a lower-end product versus a break-the-bank, top-of-the-line unit.

It's not necessary to purchase an item or items from every category in order to have a complete and functional studio. The gear in some categories covers a number of functions, eliminating the need to spend money on other equipment, and some categories fall under the "nice to have, but optional" heading, depending on what you're trying to accomplish.

Nor is it necessary to purchase every single item at once in order to start working. If you're starting from scratch, put together the smallest number of items you can that will still allow you to get going making music. Then keep track of where your system is lacking functionality, and start filling in the blanks by purchasing gear in other categories.

And don't forget about used gear. Bargains abound out there. Often for the same money as you'd pay for a new piece of equipment, you can pick up a used item of even higher quality or one that offers more functionality. Of course, there are trade-offs with used gear: lack of warranty, limited manufacturer support, abuse by former owners—buyer beware!

As you're making your picks, look carefully at your current needs and try to speculate a bit as to what the future holds. The goal is to avoid spending money twice; buy the right thing now, and you won't have to upgrade or replace the product when next year's model comes out or when your engineering and musical skills improve and warrant better gear.

Which brings me to my final point: It's a great time to be putting a studio together, or for upgrading or expanding an existing rig. The equipment on today's market is of high quality, choices are plentiful in every category, and prices are at an all-time low. The old cliché, "It's not what you've got, but how you use it," has never been more applicable.

Mixers

The mixer is the nerve center of the recording studio. Whether you've got one keyboard, a completely MIDI-synth-based rig, a computer-based hard disk recorder, or a hybrid tape/computer/MIDI rig, the mixer is where you combine and route audio signals and feed your effects boxes, mixdown recorders, and studio monitors.

As you're choosing your mixer, take a look at the number of input channels you'll need. Do you need all mono ins, or are you mainly mixing stereo keyboard outputs? How many microphones do you want to record at once? You'll need that many mic preamps. (Remember that just because a mixer doesn't have XLR connectors doesn't mean it's lacking mic preamps. Balanced and unbalanced ¼" connectors can also serve as mic inputs.) Do you need tape returns, or are all your tracks combined inside a computer-based system, requiring only a stereo output? Estimate the total number of channels you'll need, then add a few extra for good measure; it's the rare studio that doesn't grow. If you plan for expansion now, you won't have to buy a bigger mixer next year.

Once you've sussed out your input needs, consider how many outputs you'll need to feed at once. Just because you have an eight-track recorder doesn't mean you need an eight-bus console (although extra busses can serve other functions besides just feeding a multitrack). Don't forget to look at the number of aux sends and returns you'll need for connecting your reverbs and effects processors.

How much EQ do you really need? If all your inputs are coming from keyboards and samplers, your EQ needs may be fairly modest; high and low shelving may cover it. If you're trying to compensate for poor mics, instruments, voices, or room acoustics, more powerful EQ may be called for; an EQ section on each channel with one or two sweepable mids should do the job.

The Mackie MS1402-VLZ mixer is a common choice for smaller home studios.

As you're shopping, look for a mixer that fulfills your connectivity requirements, has flexible routing and EQ (if necessary), and above all, is clean. Practically every signal produced in your studio will pass through that mixer at least once, and probably several times during the course of a project. Because of this, I'd sacrifice extra bells and whistles for a cleaner signal path every time. How can you tell how clean the board is? Check out the specs to start with, but the best test is to use your ears: Does the mixer hiss when the faders are pushed up but there's no gear connected to its

Behringer's Eurorack MX2642 offers lots of connections and flexibility.

inputs? (Every component has some self-noise, but you should have to listen carefully to hear it, especially if only a few faders are raised.) Do the highs sound veiled, or is the midrange edgy? Does the bass seem tight, or is it mushy? Try to listen to signals you're familiar with using speakers you know well.

In the old days budget mixers were, shall we say, less than stellar performers. But the times have changed. Modestly priced mixers can now perform very well, with transparent sound, flexible routing and EQ, plenty of ins and outs, and low noise. You won't, in general, get the "sonic signature" that you would with a high-end "name" console, but the signals will get through in great shape, and you can always add sound-shaping outboard gear later if you find yourself wanting extra character in your audio.

Monitors

Monitors (speakers, in studio-speak) are critical components in the studio. After all, if you can't hear the audio you're working with clearly and accurately, you're going to be in big trouble! Yes, you can do quite a bit of work using headphones, but most engineers and musicians find that relying solely on headphones is less than ideal.

As with all categories of gear, the types and numbers of available monitors have expanded greatly. You can choose either passive monitors, which require a separate

Event's 20/20bas studio monitors are active, offering 130 watts to the woofer and 70 watts to the tweeter.

KRK K-RoK studio monitors are passive, meaning they require an external amplifier.

amplifier (or amplifiers), or powered (active) monitors that contain built-in power amplification. You can also choose to augment your "regular" monitors with a subwoofer—a type of speaker dedicated to extending the low-frequency (bass) response of a small monitoring system. If you're mixing for surround sound applications, or thinking of getting into surround sound, a good subwoofer that matches well with your chosen full-range monitors is essential.

If your needs are more modest, space is at a premium, or you're doing mainly Web audio work, a set of computer speakers may be just what you need. Lots of models are available; look for a set that provides the sound you want at a size that works for you.

Active (self-powered) monitors are all the rage these days, and for good reason. Combining the power amplifier, crossover, and speakers into one package is efficient, and the manufacturer can carefully match the response of each component to those of the others.

Does this mean that passive monitors (without built-in power) are a thing of the past? No way; passive monitors are as popular as ever. Many people like choosing their own size and type of power amplifier, and it's generally less expensive to upgrade just your speakers or just your amplifier than it is to replace an active monitoring system.

Most budget studios rely on direct- or close-field monitors; the speakers are relatively small, and usually positioned just a few feet from the listener. Because of this close proximity to your ears, make sure that the monitors you're considering are listenable for long periods of time, and won't cause ear fatigue. Is the midrange harsh? Are the highs edgy or overly brilliant? There's nothing worse than sitting for hours listening to harsh-sounding speakers!

Don't rely too heavily on specs when choosing your speakers. The standards manufacturers use when measuring their specs vary wildly, so direct comparisons are often almost impossible. As an example, I've seen some monitor frequency response specs cited at the –1dB point, some at –3dB, and some at the –10dB point—there's no way you can make a comparison based on those kinds of variances!

So how do you compare? The only solution is to use your ears. Despite the fact that all manufacturers claim their speakers are "flat," which means that there are no large peaks or dips in the frequency response, every model listed here sounds different from the others. (Who knows what "flat" sounds like, anyway?) The important thing is that mixes created on your monitors transfer well to other systems. There are two things that affect this: How accurate the monitors are, and even more important, how well you know the sound of your monitors and the room you're mixing in. Regardless of whether you choose an active or passive system, plan to spend a lot of time listening to them before you ever try to do a mix on them. I have a stack of favorite reference CDs that I always use to familiarize myself with monitoring systems and rooms.

If you're going for passive monitors, don't skimp on amplifier power. It's a common misconception that too much power is what damages speakers. In fact, the opposite is true: Under-powering speakers with a weak amp can result in tweeter-frying distortion that will blow your speakers every time. Don't worry about matching power amp wattage to speaker power ratings. Go for a generous amount of clean power, and avoid pushing your amplifier hard. For most studio applications, you'll also want to avoid power amplifiers with built-in cooling fans—the sound of the fans adds to the background noise in the studio, making critical listening more difficult.

Microphones

If you're working with acoustic instruments or vocals, then at some point a microphone is going to figure into your studio purchase plans. Go for the best you can. Think of the mic as the source of the audio; if you start with a great signal, it'll only get better as you polish and enhance it with the rest of your system. But if the signal starts life out on the wrong side of the tracks due to a poor microphone, there's going to be a limited amount you can do to improve the signal further down the line. You can never have too many mics; each has its own sound and applications. My advice is to start off with a good general-purpose mic, one that will cover a lot of bases for you. As you're working on projects, note which applications that mic isn't sounding its best on, and start looking for other mics that might cover those requirements better.

There are two basic types of mics to consider: dynamic and condenser. Dynamic mics use a magnetic moving-coil arrangement similar to a speaker working in reverse. Because they're electro-mechanical devices, they tend to be less sensitive and more durable than other mic types. You'll often find dynamic mics in front of electric guitar amps, horns, drums, and other loud, punchy signals.

The Shure SM58 dynamic microphone is a standard on stage, but it works great in the studio, too.

The AKG C1000S condenser microphone is a flexible, good-sounding model at an affordable price.

The AKGC414 is a studio-standard condenser mic offering multiple, switchable polar patterns.

Condenser mics don't use a moving coil of wire; they're based around changes in capacitance (capacitors are also known as "condensers," hence the name). Because of this, they can be built lighter, making them more sensitive to detail and high frequencies. Condensers are often used on quieter, more delicate acoustic instruments and vocals. Note that condensers require a power source to operate; some have built-in batteries, but most require power from an external supply. That's what a mixer's phantom power is for.

Ideally, you'd have both dynamic and condenser mics in your collection. If you must choose only one, I'd opt for a condenser. It will work fine on drums and electric guitars (be a bit careful of volume levels), and will excel on more delicate sounds.

What about polar (pickup) patterns? Mics are available in a variety of patterns, and some mics can even switch between different patterns. In the end, though, something like 90% of all recordings are made with cardioid-patterned mics. Especially in home studios, where room acoustics are often suspect, a directional mic—a cardioid—is a good choice. As your collection expands (and it will), consider adding an omni-patterned mic for its balanced, open sound and ability to capture room ambience along with the direct signal.

Effects

Effects are the icing on the cake. They're the spice that's added to a signal to enhance it or to make it sit correctly in the mix. When we refer to effects, we're talking about delay and echo, chorus, enhancers, and of course, reverb. While you can certainly do a lot of great work with just one multi-effects processor, it's nice to have at least a couple. When I'm mixing,, I always try to have one unit I can dedicate to reverb, and (at least) one other that will be used for other effects.

When choosing a reverb, look for a unit that has a number of algorithms (halls, plates, rooms, auditoriums, and so on). Every mix calls for a slightly different reverb sound, and you'll want your processor to cover them all. Listen for the quality of the "tail," or decaying portion of the reverb. Is it smooth, or does it get grainy, with fluttering noises appearing as it dies out? Does the reverb have a metallic quality, or is it warm and smooth? (Don't completely discount the unit if it does sound slightly

The Lexicon MPX100 effects processor is easy to use and relatively inexpensive, and it provides a number of high-quality effects, including reverb.

metallic; that sound works very well in certain situations.) How editable are the patches? At a minimum, look for variable reverb time, some kind of tone shaping (EQ or filters), and variable predelay. Some engineers consider editable diffusion essential in a reverb. If the unit has ROM presets only, or limited edit parameters, how useful are the presets? Do they cover what you need? Be sure to run some different sounds through the unit to check how it responds. What works well on a vocal might not sound that great on a snare drum.

I don't consider balanced connections to be essential on an effects unit. Most processors end up patched into the effects send/returns of a mixer, which are rarely balanced.

As you're choosing your effects, don't forget about stompboxes. While normally considered guitar effects, many current models are capable of multi-effects, and are of high enough quality to use in studio applications—plus, their price is usually very attractive.

Multitrack Personal Studios

Multitrack personal studios, whether digital (hard disk or MiniDisc) or analog (cassette) based, can be one of the best values out there for a budget studio. Combining a mixer, multitrack recorder, possibly effects, and other features into one reasonably

priced unit can be a great way to save money over purchasing separate pieces of gear with similar functionality. While the initial investment might seem larger compared to buying gear piece by piece, in the end, the bang for the buck quotient of personal studios ranks very high.

The Korg D8 personal digital studio offers eight tracks of recording to its internal hard disk.

Should you go digital or analog? If the main issue is price, analog is still less expensive. If your main concern is sound quality, digital is hard to beat. Cassette-based units sound very good these days, but can't match the clarity and cleanliness of digital. Digital also gives you the ability to edit your tracks.

As you're considering these units, start with the number of tracks you'll need. Can you get by with four, or do you need eight? Maybe you'll need 12 or even more to realize your musical visions. Keep in mind that many of these studios will allow you to bounce (combine) tracks together to free up space for new tracks, effectively giving you more tracks at no extra charge. Bouncing on analog tape is guaranteed to degrade the sound quality, however.

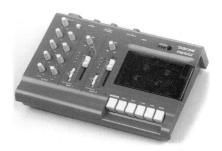

The TASCAM Porta02 Ministudio multitrack is a very inexpensive cassette-based unit.

Once you've settled on the number of tracks you need, consider how many tracks you need to record at once. Most units will do at least two. Some will do four or more. If you have one mic, and you'll be overdubbing the added parts, two simultaneous record tracks will probably be plenty. If you're miking up a drum kit with several mics, you'll likely need more simultaneous record tracks.

Consider how many mixer channels you'll need. Will you be bringing MIDI-generated synth and sampler tracks into the unit along with the tape tracks, or will everything go to tape and then be mixed down? If the latter, you'll need as many mixer channels as you have tape tracks. If the former, you'll want as many inputs as you can get.

Next consider which bells and whistles you'll need. Do you need to be able to edit tracks? How about onboard effects (which save buying an external unit)? How much EQ do you need? MIDI gear tends not to need much equalizing; acoustic instruments and vocals may need more and often benefit from a sweepable midrange EQ design.

Some personal multitrack studios contain hard drives or other storage media; others don't. Prices of options like storage and backup can add up, especially with digital systems. Shop carefully, and be sure you know what you're getting.

Stereo Mixdown Recorders

Once you've created your masterpieces, you'll want to mix them down to a medium you can take around to play for others, as well as create archives of your work and put together mixes for possible release. Most studios mix down to a stereo recorder of some sort, whether cassette, DAT (digital audio tape), MiniDisc, or, increasingly, compact disc. (While stand-alone CD recorders remain fairly pricey, computer-based CD-R burners have dropped in price and have the advantage of serving as data-backup drives. If you're using a computer-based audio system, definitely give them a look.)

If your main concern is being able to take your mixes around and play them for other people, mixing down to a good cassette deck is still a viable way to go; very few people outside of studios have DAT machines! While you can use any garden-variety home stereo cassette deck for mixdown, you'll find that a "pro" unit will often be more durable, and may have flatter and wider frequency response. Pro cassette decks are also often rackmountable, a convenient feature for many studios.

MiniDisc offers the benefits of clean digital recording, combined with random access song locating—great for live performance situations where you're playing along with backing tracks. The downsides: Despite the hype, the format has never really taken off. Playback will probably be limited to your studio, and MiniDisc isn't a commonly accepted master format at CD duplication houses.

DAT is widely used in pro studios for its great sound quality, portability, and stability. DATs are also accepted by most CD manufacturing houses, should you want to press your music and release it. As with MiniDisc, the downside is that virtually the only place you'll be able to play your tracks will be in studios. Many studios find the best solution is to mix to DAT for best sound quality, then to have a cassette deck around for making dubs you can listen to in your car, give to friends, or send to your mother.

The ART Tube Pac tube compressor/mic preamp combines a microphone preamp and compressor into one compact package.

Mic Preamps

Many mixers already have built-in microphone preamps; why would anyone want to spend money on an external unit? For two reasons: First of all, the quality of the preamps that a manufacturer builds into a mixing console may be compromised by economic considerations. They may skimp on the preamps (especially if the board has a lot of them) in order to hit a price point. Second, and far more important, the mic preamp is a major contributor to the tone and quality of the signal produced by the microphone. Mics generate extremely low voltages; it takes a very clean and accurate amplifier (a preamp is really just a type of amp) to raise that signal to a level a mixer or other device can deal with. In the process of amplifying the mic's output, the preamp may impart a certain, often sought-after, coloration to the signal. That's what makes old Neves and other vintage preamps so cool; they have a "sound" to them. Tube preamps take this concept to the extreme, often radically warming and fattening the mic's raw signal.

At the other end of the spectrum are preamps that impart no coloration; the so-called "straight-wire" approach. These units are revered for their accuracy, especially for classical and delicate acoustic recordings. The preamps in most budget consoles fall more into this camp, imparting little coloration to the signal.

Which type you'll want depends on what you're trying to achieve. The ideal situation would be to have an assortment of preamps, each with a different sound, at your disposal. Since most of us don't have that option, if you decide you need a separate mic pre to augment your mixer, look at the kind of sound you're most often trying to get. If you go for fat, warm sounds, look at a tube or vintage-style solid-state design (also a good choice if you already have clean preamps in your mixer). But keep in mind that warmth and "fat" often have a price; the preamps that produce those sounds may be noisier, and they'll certainly be less accurate than other designs. The rule is: You can always add warmth with other processing gear (say, a tube compressor or EQ) but you can never take it out of the signal once it's recorded.

Dynamics Processors and EQ

Sound-shaping processors like compressors, limiters, and equalizers can be invaluable to an engineer. Since most mixers have some form of EQ built-in, you'll probably only need an external unit if you have *serious* tone-shaping to do, or for putting the final response curve on a song as it goes to mixdown. If you need to get in and really tweak a sound or make corrections to its tone—tonal surgery— you'll want to consider a parametric EQ, which gives you control over the frequency, bandwidth, and amount of EQ applied to each frequency band. Using a parametric EQ effectively can take some practice; that much power can create as many problems as it solves.

A graphic EQ, on the other hand, is well suited to quickly shaping the overall tone of an instrument or mix. Graphic EQs also have the advantage of giving you some visual feedback on what you're doing to the signal (the curve of the slider positions on the EQ sort of resembles its response).

Most studios find a need for dynamics processing before they need an outboard EQ. Compression, in particular, is an integral part of many recordings. Look for a compressor that offers a good range of ratios, from 1:1 to 10:1 or even ∞:1 (limiting). But remember that in most cases, unless you're limiting, you'll probably be working in the 2:1 to 6:1 range. If you're inexperienced with compressors, check out one of the units that offers an automatic attack/release time setup. These critical settings can be challenging to get right, and having the compressor set them for you while you get your ears around the various sounds can be a great benefit. If you're experienced with compressors, don't completely discount the automatic models. For quick and easy processing, they're tough to beat.

Other things to look for: Fast attack times are nice for controlling peaks, while slower attacks will let you use the compressor for tone shaping as well as level control. A sidechain or trigger input lets the compressor serve as a de-esser and ducker in addition to its regular duties controlling levels. A built-in gate can be a godsend. Compression has a tendency to raise the noise floor of a signal, and having a gate to clean out the hiss is a great feature.

What about stand-alone noise gates? For most home studios, gates will be of limited usefulness, unless you have a lot of background noise when you're recording, or you're tracking multiple instruments at the same time, in the same room. Gates can, of course, also be used for other applications.

If you're looking to warm up or fatten your tracks, consider a tube-based compressor or EQ. While not as clean, nor often as accurate, as a solid-state unit, tube designs definitely will impart a certain character to the signal.

One note: If you're working with a digital personal studio or a computer-based hard disk recording system, you may be able to handle dynamics and EQ processing with software plug-ins and DSP. (See page 75 for more on plug-ins and software processing.)

The Alesis NanoSynth synthesizer module may be the world's smallest synthesizer.

Synths and Samplers

For most of us, synths and samplers are primary sound generators in our studios. Until recent years, a budget keyboard or sampler meant a cheesy consumer model with built-in speakers purchased from a stereo or department store. That's no longer the case; many companies have recognized the need for good-sounding, powerful instruments at an affordable price. And even the cheesy consumer models have gotten pretty impressive.

Most of the action is taking place with sound modules, although a few high-quality keyboards have appeared in the sub-$1,000 price range. Look for a unit that has sounds you like and plenty of polyphony to cover the parts you need. If you're sequencing, look for multitimbral support (the ability to simultaneously play different sounds on each MIDI channel). A few of the models in this price range are focused on particular types of sounds, but most are general-purpose, covering a broad range of timbres.

If you're a computer user, don't forget the new wave of software synths and samplers. Offering great bang-for-the-buck, these programs use the computer hardware you already own to generate sounds and play back samples. Plus, you get the ergonomic benefit of being able to control and edit the instrument using the computer screen rather than a limited LCD.

If you're on a budget, you'll find the most compromises with this category of gear. You won't get a disk drive, a weighted keyboard action, or other high-end features. But you will get some nice extras compared to older models. For example, many of the new units have built-in ports for connecting to a PC or Mac, eliminating the need for a separate MIDI interface. Plus, the sound quality of modern budget synths is surprisingly good—comparable to what higher-priced models sounded like only a few years ago.

The Alesis SR-16 drum machine provides great drum sounds and flexible rhythm programming.

Drum Machines

If you're not working with a sequencer, a drum machine may be a very important purchase. It's tough to record acoustic drums in most home studios. Even if you can physically manage the task, getting a good sound will still be difficult. A drum machine provides an easy solution, at least for creating demos and composing. If you feel the need to add live drums, you can always do so at a later point.

Look for a model with a good selection of sounds you like—if the sounds don't do it for you, all the bells and whistles in the world aren't going to help. Having a ton of programmable patterns and songs is great, but for studio use most people rarely use more than ten or 20 patterns to make up a song, and rarely have more than a couple of songs in memory at once. Regarding memory: Take a look at how the machine accommodates backing up and reloading user data into memory. In other words, what do you do when you've filled up the onboard RAM? Most machines will transmit their memory contents via MIDI, but doing this will require that you have a sequencer or MIDI data storage device handy.

Groove Boxes

The world of modern pop music relies more on rhythm than ever before—as evidenced by the current popularity of dance styles, and the cross-pollination of dance-influenced rhythms into everything from rock to rap to country music.

"Getting your groove on" means different things to different musicians and engineers and—depending on what you're doing and trying to accomplish—the tools used to add rhythm and percussion can vary just as widely. In some cases, what's needed is a drum machine, which is generally oriented toward those who want a "drummer in a box." A drum machine includes percussion sounds (often a *lot* of percussion sounds) as well as the ability to program drum patterns and fills using those sounds and to string those patterns and fills together to create complete rhythm tracks for songs. Drum machines can be heard in virtually all styles of music, from country to rap to jazz to the latest heavy metal styles.

Groove boxes, on the other hand, tend to be found more in the world of dance and electronic music. These devices can often fulfill some of the functions of a drum machine, but their main thrust is working with looped audio material to create rhythmic tracks. In addition, groove boxes may provide support for sampling and for recording and editing basic audio tracks—some groove boxes are so full-featured that they can almost be considered self-contained groove *studios*.

But not all rhythm tracks are coming from machines these days; percussion controllers played by "real" players are as popular as ever. You'll find manufacturers producing everything from controllers that emulate ethnic hand drums and marimbas, as well as unique percussion-based alternate controllers and complete drumset controllers. If you're a drummer or percussionist who uses one of these types of controllers—or if you're a keyboardist or programmer who regularly uses percussion sounds—you'll definitely want to check out the dedicated rhythm and percussion sound modules on the market today.

MIDI Interfaces

MIDI interfaces have one main purpose in life: To allow transfer of MIDI data in and out of a computer. To this end, they're pretty simple devices (at least operationally); plug them in and they work. As you move up the interface food chain, things get slightly more complex with multiple ins and outs, routing capabilities, and sync support, but in the budget studio things are largely straightforward.

Look at the number of ins and outs the interface has. Keep in mind that you can always daisy-chain MIDI modules from one another, so the fact that an interface has only one in and out may not be a severe limitation. But if you have a large number of devices, extra MIDI ports on the interface can come in handy.

On the Mac, your choices are straightforward: Interfaces plug in to the computer's serial (printer or modem) ports, or on the new Macs and iMacs, a USB port.

On the PC, you have a few extra options. The interface can be an internal expansion card (which occupies a slot) or an external box connected to a serial, parallel, or USB port. With external interfaces on either computer platform, look for a "thru" switch that will allow you to connect other serial or parallel devices to the computer without disconnecting the interface.

The Roland UA-100 computer audio interface connects to the computer via USB.

Computer/Audio Interfaces

Getting audio in and out of computers with decent quality has recently become a goal of many home/project studio owners. Once the audio is inside the computer, an incredible amount can be done with it. A number of manufacturers have risen to the challenge of providing the hardware support for those chasing this goal. While

The Event Gina computer audio interface uses a computer-based PCI and as well as an external breakout box.

this provides a large number of choices for you, it can also make reaching a decision on which one to buy a real dilemma.

My advice is to approach the decision methodically. Start with your computer platform. Next examine your computer to determine what kind of slots or connection possibilities you have. On the Mac, older machines will have NuBus slots; more current models will have PCI format slots. There are a few USB audio interfaces on the market, and FireWire interfaces are just becoming available at this writing. FireWire and USB have the advantage of not requiring a slot inside the computer; just connect a cable from your computer's FireWire or USB connector to the similar connector on the interface, and you're happening—no need to open up your computer and install a card.

On the PC, older machines will have ISA/EISA slots, while newer computers will have PCI. Some current models support both ISA/EISA and PCI. Some new PCs have also implemented USB and FireWire support.

Once you've determined which interfaces are physically compatible with your computer, look at the audio connector situation. Do you need only analog connections to interface your audio gear with the card, or are you also intending to use digital? If you will be using digital, which formats do you need? Cards are available that support AES/EBU, coaxial S/PDIF, optical S/PDIF, and ADAT optical.

If you're working with analog connections, how many do you need? How many inputs will you be sending into the interface at once? How many outputs do you require? If you'll be mainly overdubbing tracks one at a time, and mixing down within the computer, you can probably get by with a two-in/two-out interface. As with mixers, keep an eye toward the future, planning for possible expansion of your system. Few people regret having an extra input or output or two on their interface.

Beyond the basic parameters listed above, look at any bells and whistles the interface might have. Some support direct connection of guitars and mics, others have headphone outputs, and a few even offer built-in MIDI interfaces. Make a list of what you need, and what the potential interfaces will do, and it should be fairly easy to at least narrow your choices down.

PC Soundcards

For computer-based studio jockeys, there's another option besides a dedicated audio interface: the soundcard. A soundcard differentiates itself from an audio interface by providing a built-in synthesizer in addition to audio capabilities. This makes for a very economical package—as with personal multitrack studios, soundcards can be a cost-effective way to get your studio up and running.

As you're looking at soundcards, the same concerns apply as with audio interfaces and synthesizers. What kinds of computer slots and audio connectors are supported? How much polyphony and how many multitimbral parts does the card offer? Are there built-in effects and mixing?

And, very important, how's the quality of the synthesized sounds? Recently a number or semi-pro and pro cards have been released that have dramatically better sounds than the consumer-grade cards packaged with PCs. Having said that, don't completely discount consumer models such as the various SoundBlasters and their brethren. Many consumer cards have reasonable sound quality, and may even have digital I/O and other higher-end features. It pays to give the card a good listen before making your choice.

who's afraid of hard disk?

Put your computer to work in your studio

BY MITCH GALLAGHER

if you've been to a studio or cracked open a music technology magazine lately, you've probably noticed that personal computers are being used everywhere that music is being produced. The era of desktop audio and music creation is upon us—and what a cool era it is! Musicians now have unprecedented power and capabilities at their fingertips. Given a reasonably powerful PC or Mac, a computer-based hard disk recording system, and a few peripherals such as mics and monitors, you truly can produce a pro-quality CD right on your desktop—with few if any compromises. And even better, the price is right! When you consider what it would cost to outfit a studio with enough dedicated hardware to produce a pro-quality recording, the price of a computer, a hard disk recording system, and a few extra toys pales in comparison.

Do you have to be a pencil-necked geek to operate all that computer junk? Not at all—the software manufacturers have worked hard to make their products usable, and little hardware knowledge is required. If you can figure out how to work the computer's power switch and which finger to use to click the mouse button, odds are you can be up and running with a hard disk system in just a few hours. I'm not saying no work will be involved, just that it's nowhere near as difficult as some technophobes seem to think it is.

Why Bother?

Why should you care? Why should you get into all this computer-based stuff? A better question is, "Why in the world *shouldn't* you?" You'll gain complete control over the production of any music you want to record: From recording to editing to mastering and burning a finished CD, you can do it with your computer. There are a number of very cool benefits to making the move to a hard disk recording system:

- **Random Access.** No waiting for tape to rewind or fast-forward. Jump right to the part of the song you want to work on. Considering the limited time most of us have for our music, any seconds saved are a blessing.

- **User Interface.** Computer-based systems let you see whatever you want or need on the big screen—no need to guess or go by a tape counter. Everything's right there: mixer, recorder, editor, effects, etc.

- **Open-ended.** You're limited only by your computer's power. Need another track? A few mouse clicks and you're happening (try that with an analog recorder). If you ever run out of tracks, there are easy and sonically clean workarounds.

- **Audio Editing.** This is probably the biggest benefit to working with a hard disk-based system. Copy a verse and paste it later in the song. Delete the singer talking during the quiet acoustic guitar intro. Record a few takes of a part, then cut and paste the tracks together to quickly create a "comp" part (this took an amazing amount of time and skill in the old analog tape days). Clean up a great take, or create a completely new part using other material. Fine-tune your production until you're thrilled with every aspect of it (just don't tweak it so much that it loses all its feel and character). The beautiful thing about all this editing is that it's *non-destructive*—you can always hit the Undo button and get back to where you started.

- **Audio Processing.** Pitch-shift a part without affecting its sound quality. Slow a tempo down without changing the pitch. Add reverb, compression, EQ, and other effects all in the digital domain, and with precise control using graphic interfaces. Bounce tracks together without adding *any* noise or degradation. As with audio editing, you can usually undo any processing you might have done— a nice safety net to have.

- **System Integration.** With the advent of viable software synthesizers and samplers, the explosion of plug-in availability, and the recent increases in computer power, it's now possible to put most of your studio into your computer. No need for much extra "outside" gear at all. Besides the savings in space, wiring, and complexity, there's a big cost savings, too.

- **Automation.** When it's time to mix, you'll have unbelievable control over volume levels, panning, effects parameters, and more. It's a few seconds' work to accomplish things that would be virtually impossible on a hardware mixer/recorder system—even one that had moving fader automation built-in.

- **Ready to Burn.** If you have a CD-R drive connected to your computer, the files you create on your computer can be burned directly to a standard audio CD ready for duplication. Then use the CD-R to create backups of your precious files on CD-ROM discs. When that's done, use the computer to print labels for the CDs you've just burned. Then print out a newsletter to send to your mailing list, balance the band's checking account, jump up to your Web site to see how many people have downloaded your latest opus—that computer can do a *lot* for your music career besides serving as an audio production miracle.

Yes, there can be "techy" aspects to dealing with a computer-based system. Don't let this deter you—most people find that they can get up and running in a short time. The big hassle used to be installing the hardware and software. The newer "plug-n-play" operating systems have largely removed the pain from this process—most devices and programs have easy-to-follow installation directions, and things go smoothly. If you're concerned about rooting around inside your computer to install an audio interface card, call in a favor from a computer-savvy friend or—easier yet—go for a USB- or FireWire-based audio interface that doesn't require you to open your computer up at all (assuming your computer supports USB or FireWire connections).

Audio software has also gotten more user-friendly. Most musicians I've watched can sit down and get a track recorded in a matter of minutes—it's usually as easy as choosing a track, arming it to record (just as you would an ADAT or analog tape deck), setting levels, and hitting the record button.

What's It Going to Take?

There are three parts to a hard disk recording system: The computer, the audio interface, and the software. If you already own a reasonably modern computer, you're in good shape. If not, you'll need to do some shopping. Just about any computer you find in the stores these days will be plenty fast enough for audio production. Just be sure you get a large enough hard drive (as big as possible is the usual recommendation, but at a minimum you can get by with a few gigabytes free) and enough RAM (too much is never enough). You'll also want to check that the computer you have or buy is completely compatible with the hardware and software you want to run. Check with the software manufacturer for their recommendations on compatible audio interfaces and minimum computer hardware requirements; don't buy based on assurances from a computer superstore salesperson who has never used the particular audio program you're planning to use.

Choosing the best audio interface and software is a bit trickier, since every manufacturer seems to have their own idea of what you need to effectively produce your music. While the hardware and software for hard disk recording are sometimes bundled together, usually you'll buy them separately.

The hardware consists of an audio interface; this can be as simple as a single card that plugs into your computer's expansion slot, or as complex as a rig consisting of multiple computer cards and rackmount converter boxes. Prices range from a few hundred dollars to $50,000 or more. (If you're in the former price range, don't worry, you can still get great results. If you're in the latter category, well, you don't need to worry, either . . . .)

The easiest way to decide on which audio interface to buy is to sit down and figure out what your needs are: How many inputs will you need? How many outputs? If you work largely on your own, two or four inputs may be all you'll need. If you want to record a full band simultaneously, look for an interface with as many inputs as possible. A digital input can be useful for transferring audio off of DAT or from some digital processors and synths/samplers with digital connections.

You'll need a pair of outputs for your main stereo mix. If you want a separate headphone monitor mix, or you want to have outputs to use as effects sends (as you would on a stand-alone mixer) allow for a few extra outs. A digital out is very useful for mixing down to DAT machines and for interfacing with some effects processors.

Other things to consider: Do you ever work with digital tape machines such as Alesis ADATs or TASCAM DA-88s? There are interfaces that can connect digitally to those tape machines, as well as sync up the computer so that the tape machine and the audio software can operate in parallel.

Are the analog-to-digital and digital-to-analog converters located on a card in the computer or in an external box? The inside of a computer is a hostile environment for sensitive audio converters; many people feel that locating those components in a separate enclosure is a good idea.

Do you want to have MIDI support built into the interface? This can be useful if you're syncing to a sequencer, or controlling effects, etc., with MIDI from your computer. You can, of course, also use a separate stand-alone MIDI interface alongside your audio interface, so this shouldn't be a deal-breaker.

Software offers just as large an array of options. The questions here: Do you need MIDI sequencing capabilities along with audio recording? How many tracks of each? How much audio editing do you want to do? Most packages will let you cut/copy/paste audio in the same way a word processor can deal with text. As you go up the ladder, the amount and types of editing will expand. Does the program support audio processing plug-ins or have realtime DSP (Digital Signal Processing)? How much of a mixer do you need? Just level control? Need EQ? Effects sends? Make a list of your requirements, and start doing some homework—the good news is that at all price levels, you can't go too far wrong; the quality out there is uniformly high.

So why bother with all this? Why not just use the soundcard that came in your PC or the built-in audio jacks on the back of your Mac—don't they claim those are "CD-quality"? Well, first of all, "CD-quality" is a pretty ill-defined term; all that really says is that the audio is running at 16-bit/44.1kHz resolution, which is fine, but it doesn't *really* tell us about the audio quality. Suffice it to say that most onboard soundcards are fine for games, Internet audio files, or quick down-and-dirty demos. For pro-quality audio, stick with a dedicated interface designed for audio production.

What's the Bottom Line?

How much will all this cost? The answer depends. Even excluding the price of the computer, the range can still be broad. On the hardware side, Emagic, Echo, Midiman/M Audio, Turtle Beach, SEK'D, Frontier Design Group, and many others offer interfaces in the under-$500 price range. For a few hundred dollars more, you can get into models from Yamaha, Mark of the Unicorn, Aardvark, and others, which offer lots of options and expandability.

If you move up to the $1,000–$1,500 price range, things open up even more; among other products, Mark of the Unicorn has their 2408 (24 ins/outs in various analog and digital formats), and its various brethren. Yamaha offers the DSP Factory, which combines expandable input and output capabilities with onboard mixing and effects power equivalent to a high-end digital mixer and effects boxes. Digidesign has their Digi 001 system, which combines a special edition of their high-end Pro Tools software with a powerful audio interface.

As you go up the price ladder from there, you'll find expanded input/output capabilities, and DSP possibilities increase, although arguably audio quality won't necessarily improve all that much (the Law of Diminishing Returns definitely applies). Even the least expensive interface mentioned above is capable of high-quality output.

Software has a similar range of prices, starting at $29 for PG Music's PowerTracks AV. For under $100, you can get into basic versions of higher-end programs. Examples include Emagic's MicroLogic AV and Steinberg's Cubasis AV. For a few dollars more, Cakewalk has their Home Studio software. And if you're a guitar player, Cakewalk has a program with features aimed specifically at you, Guitar Studio.

As you move into the higher price ranges, you'll encounter SEK'D's Samplitude, Syntrillium Software's Cool Edit Pro, and others. If you're looking for a powerful integrated MIDI sequencer/digital audio program, Cakewalk Pro Audio and SONAR, Emagic Logic Audio, Mark of the Unicorn Digital Performer, and Steinberg Cubase VST take the "studio-in-a-computer" concept to amazing heights.

Now Make It Rock

In the end, what it all comes down to is the musician and his or her music.

With hard disk recording systems, the power to produce music is now in the hands of the musicians—the tools are out there, it's just a matter of sitting down, getting to know them, and putting them to work. For me, getting into desktop audio has been one of the best things to happen to my music in a long time. I think the same will be true for you. Who says computers can't rock 'n' roll?

choosing a computer

BY MITCH GALLAGHER

n most cases, the computer you choose to host your hard disk-based recording system will have a major impact on how much you're able to accomplish. An older model might barely be able to deal with a few tracks of audio—forget about doing much equalization (EQ) or effects processing, at least from within the computer. (You'll still be able to use external hardware effects.) By contrast, a state-of-the art, fire-breathing PC will give you the raw power to literally create a complete studio-in-a-box. Here are a few things to consider as you check out computers:

MAC or PC?

For much of the past, the Apple Macintosh has ruled high-end pro audio applications. Its hold has loosened considerably, and you can now choose either Mac or a Windows PC without feeling like you're missing out. Consider whether the hard disk system you want requires Mac or PC, look at what your friends own, ask around a bit, then pick a platform. You can't really go wrong either way.

General Guidelines

The best way to choose a computer is to choose the software you'll be running *first*, then get a computer powerful enough to comfortably run it. But as general guidelines, on the Mac side, you can get started with a 200MHz 604 processor. A G3 or G4 is better. For Windows, a 200MHz Pentium is barely going to get you by these days; a Pentium II, III, or IV is better. You can certainly do a lot of creating with a less stout machine than these, but you'll find yourself more and more limited as audio applications become more powerful and demanding of host computers.

Regardless, be aware that your computer will be obsolete before you've even signed the credit card slip at the check-out counter. Don't get too gripped about this. Buy as much machine as you can, and put it to work making music. If you decide to wait for next month's faster machine, you'll never buy anything—there will always be a faster machine on the horizon.

Hard drive: Current computers just about always come with a built-in hard drive. While you can use this internal drive for recording, storing, and playing back your music, you're often better off using another, dedicated drive. At 44.1kHz/16-bit (CD) resolution, digital audio will use up five megabytes per minute per track. A 16-track production will eat up 80MB per minute—and that's without any alternate takes, etc. Switching to 24-bit resolution will increase this by 50%, and using a higher sample rate such as 96kHz will more than double this requirement! Get as much drive space as you can. If you intend to work on large multitracked projects (more than 16 tracks), get the fastest drive and interface you can (Ultra ATA or Ultra SCSI). Firewire is also an increasingly popular option, but I'd avoid USB hard drives for most multi-track audio work.

Memory: Go for as much RAM (Random Access Memory) as you can reasonably afford, and make sure your computer will allow you to add more memory later. I've never known anyone who felt they had too much memory in their computer. The opposite is usually the case. 32MB is the absolute bare minimum these days; 64MB is better, but still not enough for serious audio work. Many studio owners are loading their computers with up to 256 megs of RAM, and some even go higher. If you're going to be running software samplers that store their sounds in the computer's memory, factor this into the total amount you'll need.

Increasing the amount of RAM in your computer is one of the best upgrade options for improving its performance.

Processor speed: You'll usually see this rated in MHz (megaHertz). All other things being equal, the higher this number, the better (*i.e.,* a 400MHz machine is better than a 266MHz machine). But don't get too gripped by how fast the processor is running. Lots of other things can impact performance, and the difference between, say, a 300MHz and a 400MHz machine isn't night and day—more like the difference between late morning and early afternoon.

Expansion slots: These are connectors inside the computer that let you install optional hardware like audio cards. Having several vacant slots is a good idea if you feel your musical needs may grow. Several types of expansion have been used by computer manufacturers, but these days the standard for both Mac and PC is PCI. Some PCs offer both ISA and PCI slots; for future compatibility I'd stick with PCI. However, lately, FireWire and USB MIDI and audio interfaces have hit the market, which don't require expansion slots at all—but they do require that the computer have appropriate FireWire or USB connectors available.

Monitor: Your computer's monitor is your window on the digital audio world—get the largest screen size you can. Most computers come with a 15-inch model these days, which you'll probably find will cramp your style (and your mouse hand). Consider upgrading to a 17-inch or even larger monitor—you won't regret it. Some studio owners equip their computers with two (or sometimes even more) monitors in the quest for as much available screen real estate as possible.

Other stuff: Printers and other peripherals are nice, and you can certainly do a lot with them. But if your main focus for the computer is music, concentrate on getting the best basic machine you can, and leave the extras for later. One exception: A modem and Internet connection is a must-have for downloading software upgrades.

software for the studio

BY MITCH GALLAGHER

many home studios are built around computers these days, and what is it that makes the computer world go 'round? You got it, *software*. A wide variety of very powerful software is available, much of it quite reasonably priced. Regardless of your needs or budget, you'll likely be able to find a program that will cover you.

You won't necessarily need software from each of the categories described below—it depends on what you want to do with your computer. If you never need to print out scores or sheet music of your songs, for example, you probably won't need a notation program. If you don't have any MIDI gear, then there's no reason to buy a MIDI editor/librarian. Evaluate your needs, and make your purchases accordingly.

If you're just putting your studio together, and aren't sure of what all you'll need, consider starting out with an integrated MIDI sequencer/multitrack digital audio program. One of these multi-faceted programs can cover a lot of bases for you. Then, as you get a better idea of the specific things you want to do, you can fill in the holes with more specialized pieces of software as necessary.

Integrated MIDI Sequencer/Digital Audio

These programs are the powerhouses of the studio world, combining a full-featured MIDI sequencer with multitrack digital audio recording, mixing, and editing. But these programs don't stop there. Many include the ability to create musical notation; they're also generally capable of serving as hosts to plug-ins, which can be used to process your audio files. (See the next chapter for more on plug-ins.)

If you're strapped for cash, scaled-down versions of the top-of-the-line programs are often available. While you won't necessarily find all the features in a budget version that you might in a top-of-the-line program, most, if not all, of these programs are capable of serving as the heart of a computer-based studio. The plus side of the trade-off with the budget versions is that they're often easier to use, require less computer power, and don't have the steep learning curves of their big brothers—a

MOTU's Digital Performer is an integrated digital audio/MIDI sequencing program. It offers almost endless MIDI and audio recording, editing, and processing features. In addition, it can display digital video—a great feature if you're scoring to picture. Digital Performer can also run plug-ins, and it offers a full-featured mixer. A program like this or its similarly equipped competitors—Emagic's Logic Audio, Cakewalk's SONAR, or Steinberg's Cubase—can offer almost everything needed to create a studio within your computer. If your needs lean mostly toward MIDI, a version of the program called "Performer" is available that's oriented primarily as a MIDI sequencer.

An integrated digital audio/MIDI program such as Emagic's Logic Audio contains almost as much functionality as a full hardware-based studio: recording, editing, processing, even software synthesizers and samplers can run within the program—as long as your computer is up to the task!

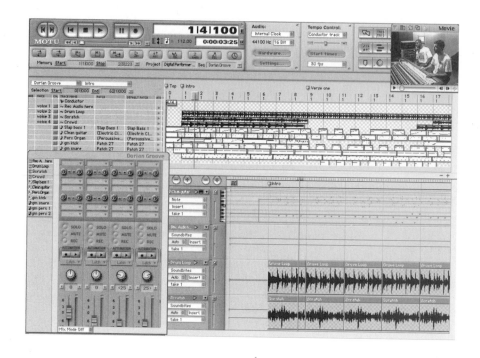

Steinberg's Nuendo offers some MIDI sequencing capability, but it's really oriented more toward working with audio. It offers a full mixer with EQ and compression on each channel as well as support for VST-format plug-ins. In addition, complete audio recording, editing, and processing is supported, as is surround sound mixdown. If you aren't working heavily with MIDI, a program such as Nuendo would make a great centerpiece for your studio.

good thing if your goal is to produce music, not to be a computer software expert. For many studios, one of these programs will be all the software you'll need.

Digital Audio

In addition to integrated MIDI sequencer/multitrack digital audio programs, there are several other types of digital audio software out there. One main type is basically a subset of the integrated programs described above: multitrack digital audio recorder/editors. When combined with a soundcard or audio interface, one of these programs can

Native Instrument's Spektral Delay is an example of a high-powered audio processing program that can run either stand-alone or as a plug-in within a host program such as Steinberg's Nuendo or Emagic's Logic Audio (among others). Spektral Delay allows you to break a sound down into many component frequency bands, then add echo processing to each of the frequency bands individually. The results have to be heard to be believed.

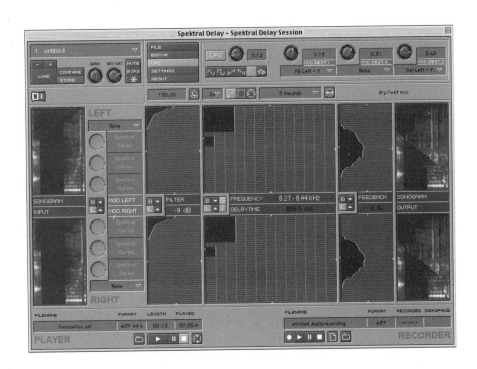

Propellerhead's Reason is a unique program: It contains software modules designed to duplicate the functionality of a studio—mixers, samplers, synthesizers, effects, equalizers, sequencers, and more. These modules can be combined however you like to create the "rack" of tools you need to produce your music. It's simple to operate, sounds great, is efficient in its use of computer power, it is reasonably cheap—and it's a blast to use!

The "rack" of modules contained in Reason can be flipped around to show its back, allowing you to "patch" or connect the modules in a particular order—just like real hardware gear!

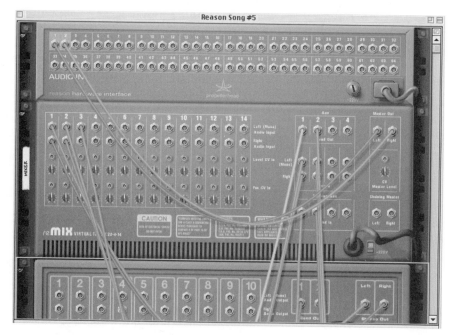

take the place of a hardware multitrack tape machine. If you won't be doing any MIDI work, one of these can serve as the centerpiece for your studio. (If you'll also be doing MIDI-based music, then you're probably better off with an integrated MIDI sequencer/ multitrack digital audio program, as described above.) In addition, there are programs designed for editing and processing samples and stereo audio files.

As remixing and loop-based music increase in popularity, a number of programs optimized toward working with those styles of music have emerged. If you plan to do a lot of work with loops, check these out. You'll find that they make the process of setting a loop to a particular tempo and key very easy.

There are also a number of programs available for accomplishing specific tasks. These include utilities for data-compressing audio files for archiving, as well as programs designed to assist with metering, noise reduction, and click/pop removal.

Software Synths and Samplers

This category of music software has emerged only recently with the incredible increases in available computer power. Software synths and samplers are software-only products that duplicate the functionality of hardware synthesizers and samplers. A variety of types have been released, including some that exactly duplicate a particular hardware model and others that break new ground, offering synthesis power never before available. Software synths and samplers can run either as "stand-alone" programs or as plug-ins within a host program. (See the next chapter for more on plug-ins.)

The big advantages are that software synths and samplers are far less expensive than similar hardware models; plus you can often run more than one "instance" of a program at once, so you can have multiple things happening at once. The limiting factor on software synths and samplers is the same as with any software-based application: your computer's power. Both the speed of your computer and the amount of RAM you have installed in your machine will affect performance variables, such as

Native Instruments' Absynth is a software synthesizer that can run either as a stand-alone application or as a plug-in within a host program. It's capable of an almost endless array of synthetic textures, both new and old.

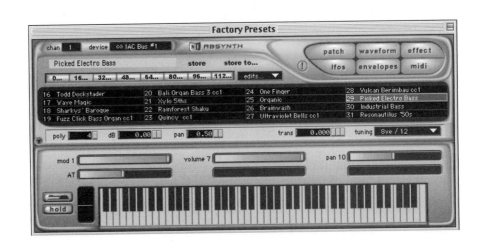

Emagic's ES1 is an analog-type soft synth that runs within the company's Logic Audio software. It provides easy sound editing and complete integration within Logic Audio.

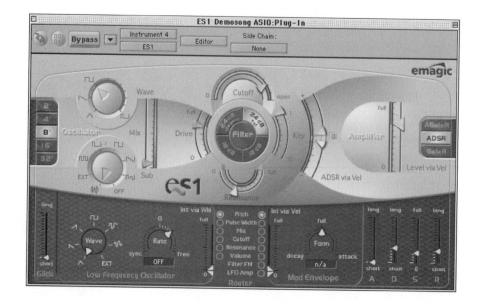

Model E, from Steinberg, is designed to emulate classic analog hardware synthesizers such as the Minimoog. It runs as a plug-in in programs such as Steinberg's Cubase and others that support the VST instrument plug-in format.

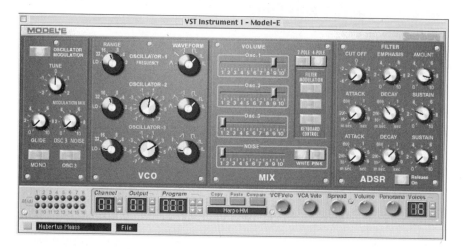

Native Instruments' Pro 52 is intended to exactly duplicate the sound and capabilities of the vintage Sequential Circuits Prophet 5 analog synthesizer. It runs either stand-alone—effectively turning your computer into a synthesizer—or as a plug-in.

the number of notes you can play at once or the number of samples you can have loaded simultaneously.

Along with processing and effects plug-ins, software synths and samplers seem to be the wave of the future. As computers continue to increase in horsepower, these programs will only get better and better and more and more capable. Given their comparatively low prices, this is *great* news for the home studio owner!

MIDI Sequencers and Auto Accompaniment

If you won't be working with computer-based audio tracks, then a MIDI sequencer may be all you need in the way of software. Also in this category are auto accompaniment programs that provide backing tracks via MIDI.

A MIDI sequencer allows you to record the MIDI data generated by a keyboard (or other MIDI controller). This data can be arranged into tracks (just as with audio): one for bass, several others for drums, maybe another for string parts, and so on. You can then edit, rearrange, and process this data in myriad ways. Keep in mind that with a MIDI sequencer, you're not recording or working with actual audio or sound; you're dealing with MIDI data, which tells a MIDI device such as a synthesizer or sampler what sound to play. Because of this, the load on the computer is much lighter than when dealing with audio data.

MIDI Editor/Librarians

In this category, you'll find programs dedicated to helping you improve the efficiency of your studio, especially your MIDI gear. Editors allow you to manipulate the

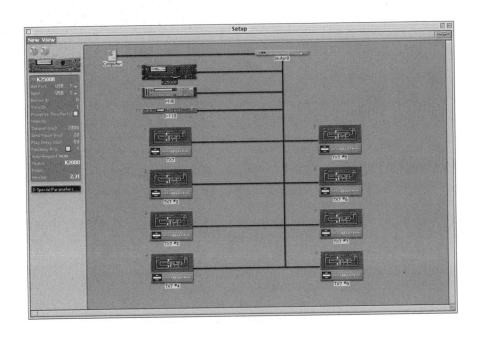

Emagic's SoundDiver is a MIDI editor/librarian. It's designed to let you manage all the synths, samplers, and MIDI-capable gear (such as effects boxes) in your studio. It can create and manage a library of all your sounds and patches, as well as help you manage MIDI routing around your rig.

Once Emagic's SoundDiver knows what MIDI gear you're using, it provides graphic editing tools that make patch programming and editing a breeze compared to using the little LCD display window on the hardware box itself.

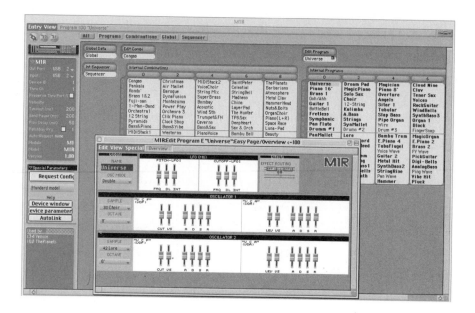

parameters of your synths and samplers via the computer screen, a distinct improvement over the small LCD displays built into most keyboards and modules. Librarians allow you to archive and organize the patches and samples you've collected for your rig, giving you quick access to any sound you might need. Many programs of this type integrate editor and librarian functions.

Notation

Notation software is dedicated to one task: Creating legible notated versions of your songs. Look for a program that allows you to enter the music by several means: playing it in from a MIDI keyboard, entering it onscreen with the mouse, using QWERTY keyboard commands, and transcribing (converting) MIDI files. Also look at the quality of the notation once it's been printed out on paper. Can you adjust and manipulate the score layout? What kinds of editing options are provided? Do you need alternate noteheads or unusual notation symbols? If you're working with guitar music, do you need tablature?

You won't find that most budget notation software can rival the tweaky notation capabilities of high-end, publishing-quality programs, but the power available in a budget program is outstanding for lead sheets, composing, rough drafts, or printing out quick scores. With a little work, you'll be able to create good-looking sheet music.

CD Burning

Being able to burn a finished audio CD of your music is an amazing accomplishment—the CD medium is so much more faithful than the audio cassettes most home

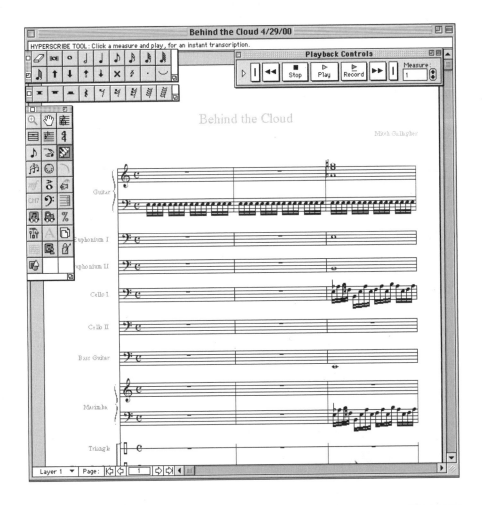

A notation program such as Coda's Finale lets you create professional-looking scores and sheet music using your computer. You can enter and edit the data from your computer keyboard, play a MIDI keyboard while the program transcribes your performance, or have the program transcribe a file imported from a MIDI sequencer.

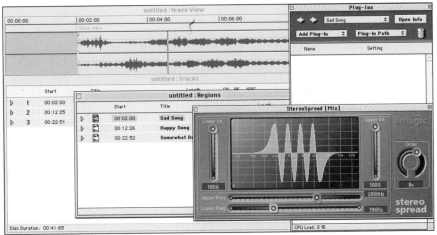

Emagic's Waveburner is an audio CD burning program. You can trim and clean up the songs, place them in different orders, change the spacing between them, use plug-ins for final sonic tweaks and sweetening, and burn a standard audio CD all from within the program.

studio owners were forced to use as recently as two or three years ago. CD burning software ranges from very simple applications that just allow you to set the order of songs, to professional-level programs that allow you to edit every aspect of the audio CD before it is sent off to a duplication plant. For simple demos or for reference listening (playing a mix on a home stereo or in a car) the former is fine. If you're after completely pro results with control over CD minutiae, the latter is what you'll need.

Beyond burning audio CDs, a CD burner can be used to back up computer data: sound files, synth patches, samples, project files, and more. In some cases, the same software you use for burning your audio CDs can be used to create data backup CDs. But if your needs reach beyond the basics, you may want to consider a more dedicated data backup program.

CHAPTER **8**

plug-in!

Extend the power of your studio with software processors and instruments

BY MITCH GALLAGHER

a plug-in is a small application that runs within a host program and extends the host's capabilities in some way. In the music world, most plug-ins are audio processors of one sort or another, although plug-in software synthesizers and samplers have become increasingly common of late. The range of plug-ins available is truly staggering, and sometimes there's surprisingly little difference between those on the high end and those in the lower price ranges. You'll give up a little control and maybe a few features, but the basics will be there, and the sound quality will usually be excellent regardless of what price you pay.

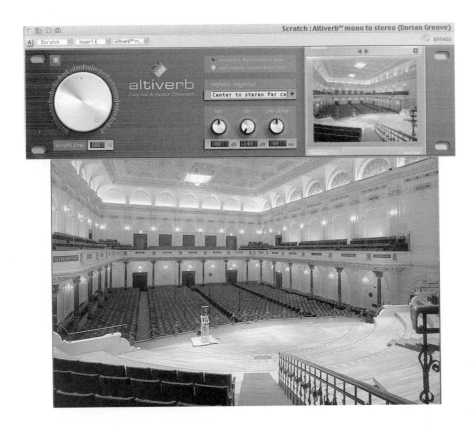

Altiverb, a MAS-format plug-in from AudioEase, creates reverb effects based on "sampling" the ambience of real, physical spaces. In fact, you can "sample" any room you like and use it to create new reverb settings in the plug-in. You can even include digital photos of the space you've sampled. If you're looking for the ultimate in realistic reverb sounds and using a MAS-compatible program such as MOTU's Digital Performer, Altiverb is a far more cost-effective solution than competing hardware processors.

While most plug-ins are designed to provide pristine audio results, Emagic's Bitcrusher plug-in, for their Logic Audio integrated digital audio/MIDI sequencer, is intended to provide the opposite. It lets you add distortion, as well as "downsample" the audio to a lower bit-resolution for convincing "lo-fi" effects.

MOTU's eVerb for MAS-compatible programs is a flexible reverb plug-in that comes bundled with the company's Digital Performer integrated digital audio/MIDI sequencing program.

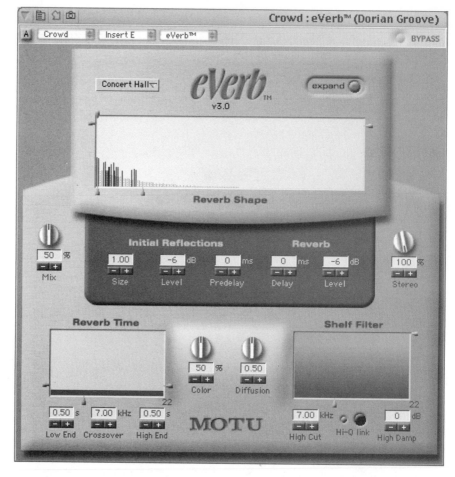

INA-GRM's GRM Tools is a suite, or bundle, of plug-ins that provide unique audio processing capabilities. Freeze, shown here, lets you capture a chunk of audio from a track and manipulate it.

Several general categories of plug-ins are available: One division is between those that require dedicated DSP chips on a soundcard, and those that don't. Those that don't are referred to as "native" since they run right on the computer's CPU. In most cases there's not that much difference between a native and a DSP-chip-based plug-in, but be aware that playing audio tracks while using native plug-ins can put a heavy load on your computer—be sure you've got a fast machine and plenty of RAM. With a chip-based plug-in, you're guaranteed that you'll have a certain amount of dedicated muscle for applying plug-ins—whether it's *enough* muscle for your needs is another question entirely. There are work-arounds if your system doesn't have enough power to run as many plug-ins as you'd like. For example, you can "bounce"—essentially re-record—a track with plug-in processing to another track, allowing you to turn off the plug-in and gain back the power it was using. This isn't as efficient as being able to run as many plug-ins as you want in real time, but it works very well.

Some plug-ins operate in real time (while the music is playing), while others are file-based (sometimes called "offline" processing), which means that you have to stop playback, apply the plug-in, wait for it to process the audio into a new file, then start the music playing again. Real-time plug-ins are desirable if your computer is powerful enough to run them, but many types of processing, such as normalizing, reversing the playback of audio files, and DC offset removal, are only available offline. Which types of plug-in you'll be using, as well as which host format you'll need, will depend on whether or not your soundcard or audio interface has built-in DSP chips and what audio software you're using. A number of stan-

Could a reverb processor get much easier to operate than this three-control plug-in from Steinberg for their Nuendo digital audio program?

Equalizer plug-ins, like this parametric version from MOTU, let you control the tone of a track with incredible accuracy.

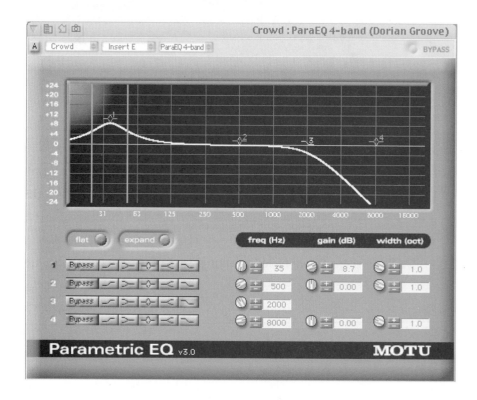

dards exist, including AudioSuite, DirectX, MAS, Premiere, TDM, and VST. New formats are still appearing, such as the recently released Digidesign RTAS (Real Time AudioSuite) format.

Plug-ins offer a cost-effective alternative to hardware gear if you're working in the computer/digital audio world. In addition, when you're using plug-ins, your audio signals remain completely in the digital domain, helping to ensure high sound quality. Before you spring for a hardware compressor or other processor or effect, take a look at what these little beauties can do—you may be surprised (and pleased) at how much power you can get for your dollars.

Some plug-ins, such as this Virsonix/BBE Sonic Maximizer, are intended to emulate a specific piece of hardware processing gear. Software companies go to extreme lengths to duplicate every aspect of the hardware piece that they are "modeling" in software.

If you're a guitar player, this VST-format plug-in from Steinberg will look familiar.

freeware and shareware

BY MITCH GALLAGHER

ooking for the best possible price on software for your studio? Some friendly programmers have your best interests at heart; these kindly souls create programs, then offer them either for free (called freeware) or as shareware. Shareware isn't free, although you may be able to acquire the software without paying for it up front. The shareware idea is that the programmer sets a reasonable (often $5, $10, or $20) price for his or her product; you're on the honor system to pay that price once you have the software in your possession. Just about any type of program can be found as either freeware or shareware: digital audio editors, sequencers, plug-ins, software synths, synth editor/librarians, you name it.

So where do you go to find these jewels? The Internet, of course! Two sites to check out are the Shareware Music Machine (www.hitsquad.com/smm), and Harmony Central (www.harmony-central.com). Each offers a wide variety of programs

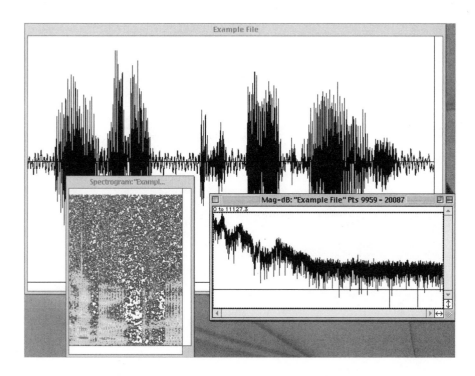

Figure 1 SoundHandle by Dave Veeneman is a freeware audio editor for the Mac that's downloadable from the Web. The program lets you perform a variety of editing and processing tasks on your audio files.

81

Figure 2 Digidesign's Pro Tools Free software is a freeware version of the studio-standard audio recording/mixing/editing software. It can be downloaded from the Digidesign Web site (www.digidesign.com) or ordered on CD-ROM for the cost of shipping. Here we see the software's mixing window, which duplicates the functionality of a hardware mixing board. Track levels can be set, channels can be routed to buses, and plug-in processors can be used to EQ, compress, or otherwise process the sound.

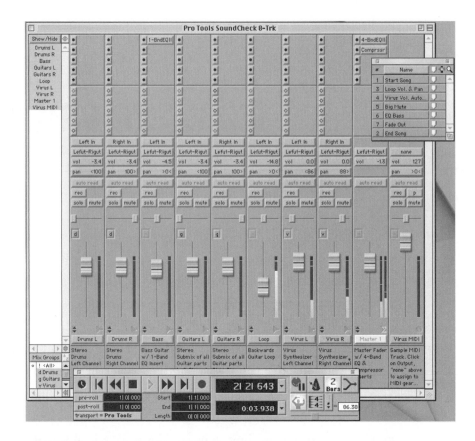

Figure 3 In Pro Tools Free's editing window, you can zoom in to cut and paste audio, move chunks of audio around, automate volume and pan levels, and much more.

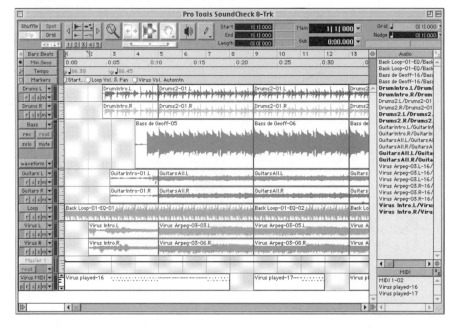

in all categories, and all of it is either free for the downloading or affordably priced shareware.

Can you expect a free or super-inexpensive program to have every bell and whistle that a high-dollar commercial release has? The answer is generally no, although you might find yourself surprised at just how much many of these programs do have to offer. The other negative is that you don't have a retailer or tech support team to fall back on if you have installation or user problems or questions. Although many freeware and shareware authors are willing to help end users, they don't have the resources that a "commercial" software company can bring to bear.

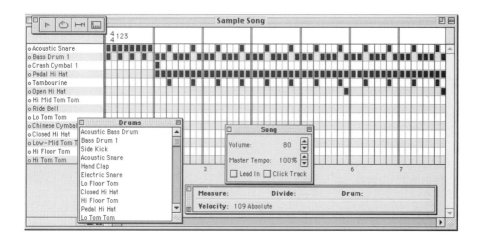

Figure 4 Jon Nichol's Virtual Drummer is a software-based drum machine for the Macintosh. It's available at www.virtualdrummer.com.

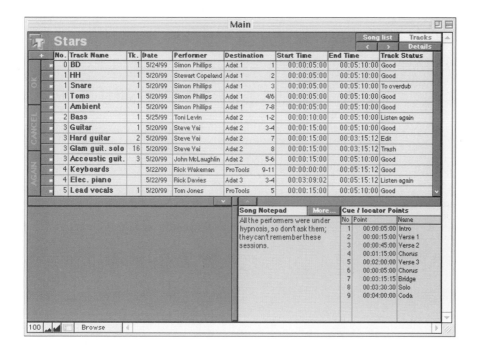

Figure 5 TrackTracker Lite from Ruidosoft (www.ruidosoft.com) is a freeware version of the company's project management software. You can create a file that lets you keep track of all elements of a project, including the tracks in each song, lyrics, notes, and more.

But that shouldn't discourage you from giving freeware and shareware a try. There are a lot of very powerful programs out there, and the price is certainly right! Just be sure to do the right thing and pay for any shareware you download and use — that way programmers will keep developing those cool (and cheap) programs for all of us.

microphone basics

BY MITCH GALLAGHER

icrophones are arguably the most fundamental of all audio components. Unless a sound is entirely electronically synthesized, it had to have been captured at some point with a microphone. Exceptions include certain musical instruments, such as electric guitars, which use other types of transducers (devices that change one type of energy, such as string vibration, into another, such as electrical current, *i.e.,* "pickups") for creating their sound, but by and large, microphones are essential tools for capturing audio.

Given how essential microphones are to just about all audio work, a basic understanding of the various types, and of microphone characteristics in general, can be very useful. Fortunately, mics aren't complex beasts. The real challenge is knowing which mic to use when, how a particular mic will sound in a certain situation, and where to place the mic for the best sound. But the first step in meeting that challenge is getting a handle on the basics. Let's dive in!

Microphone Types

Microphones can be classified according to how they operate; that is, what method they use for converting acoustic sound into electrical signals. There are two basic types of mics: dynamic and condenser.

Dynamic mics make use of electromagnetic properties to convert sound to electricity; they don't require an external power source to operate. A very thin sheet of metal-coated mylar called a "diaphragm" is attached to a coil of wire, which is placed in a magnetic field. When sound waves strike the diaphragm, the coil of wire moves in the magnetic field, creating an electric current. This electric current is then sent out of the mic to a recorder or sound system. Note that dynamic mics operate exactly opposite of how speakers work. In fact, in certain cases, it's possible to use a speaker as a microphone (albeit a poor one).

Condenser mics, on the other hand, use the electrical property of capacitance to operate. As with a dynamic mic, a metal-coated mylar diaphragm is used to "collect"

Microphone Polar Patterns

Using a number of different construction techniques, microphone manufacturers are able to control how sensitive to sound a given mic is from various directions; this characteristic is known as the mic's polar pattern (also known as its pickup pattern). By carefully selecting and positioning a mic, you can use its polar pattern to control what sound is being picked up, and what sound the mic is less sensitive to. There are a number of standard polar patterns in use today. As you select mics for your studio, think about what sounds you'll be recording, how you'll be recording them, what kind of physical space you'll be working in, and what extraneous sound you need to control. A few things to keep in mind:

- The ability of a mic to reject off-axis sound (sound not coming in the front of the mic) varies with frequency. Low frequencies are largely nondirectional in nature, and mics won't reject them very well regardless of polar pattern. Mid and high frequencies are much more directional, and mics tend to reject them better.

- Making a mic directional also makes it subject to the proximity effect, a boost in low-frequency response as the mic is brought closer to the sound source. The amount of the proximity effect increases by 6dB each time you halve the distance between the source and the mic. Typically you'll find the proximity effect becoming a factor when your source is less than one or two feet from the mic. Some mics produce up to 16dB of boost

below 100Hz when positioned very close to the sound source.

For some applications (such as vocals) proximity effect can be desirable. For applications where you want a more natural sound, proximity effect may cause problems.

- Most directional mics have ports (usually small slots) around the back of the capsule. Covering these ports makes the mic less directional. This is something to be aware of with handheld mics and mics that have been taped into place.

- The frequency response (and tone) of a directional mic changes as you move off-axis (away from directly in front of the mic). For best fidelity, position directional mics directly on-axis. If you're looking for a somewhat different tone, experiment with turning the mic off-axis slightly.

- Most of the time when we refer to a mic's polar pattern, we're actually talking about a highly simplified description of how the mic responds to off-axis sound. For more specific, detailed information on how the mic reacts to off-axis sound, you'll need to consult the mic's polar response curve (see sidebar "Polar Response Curve").

Here's a brief guide to the various polar patterns:

Omnidirectional—Picks up sound equally well from all directions. Great if you want to capture the ambient sound of a room along with the source sound being recorded. Omnis also tend to have very even frequency response, without the proximity effect (bass boost) caused by making a microphone

the sound. But in a condenser mic, the diaphragm moves in relation to a charged plate, creating changes in capacitance. ("Condenser" is another word for capacitor.) The tiny electric current that results is amplified inside the microphone, then sent out to a recorder or sound system. Because they require the extra amplification stage inside the microphone, condensers normally require an external power source,

null point

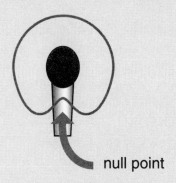

null point

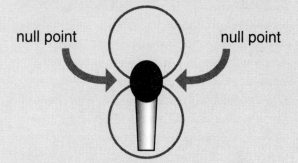

null point   null point

directional. Omnis aren't very good, however, if you're trying to control the pickup of unwanted noise.

Cardioid—The most common microphone polar pattern. The vast majority of all studio recordings are done with cardioid (also known as unidirectional) mics. Cardioids offer the best pickup from right in front of the mic, with rejection increasing as you move around to the side and a null point behind the

mic. Position the mic so that sounds to be rejected are entering the mic directly from the rear.

Hypercardioid—Similar to cardioid, but offers two null points; one at around 150 degrees and the other at around 210 degrees. This results in a slight "tail" directly behind the mic that will pick up some sound. Hypercardioids make a great choice if you're using two floor monitors on stage. Aim one monitor

into each null point, and you're set. In the studio, carefully consider where the nulls are located when trying to control sound.

Figure 8—Also known as bidirectional. Has two large pickup "lobes," one in front of and one in back of the mic. Note that the two lobes are not independ-

ent with regard to the mic's output signal (the mic only has one output)—so the figure 8 pattern is not the same as the pattern provided by a stereo mic. Best rejection is straight to the sides (90 degrees off-axis). Bidirectional patterns are useful for recording two singers at once, or if you want to capture some room ambience along with the source sound, but their polar characteristics make them less useful for many sound isolation applications.

called *phantom power*, to operate. Some condenser mics can operate off batteries, eliminating the need for phantom power.

There are actually two types of condenser mics: *electret* and *true condensers*. Electret mics tend to be less expensive; they feature a permanently charged plate. A true condenser requires power for the plate as well as for its internal amplifier. Both types require phantom power (or batteries) as described above.

Polar Response Curves

Most of us have heard the term *frequency response*, which is a description of the frequency range of a device (the span of frequencies the device can deal with) and the amplitude(s) at which it passes frequencies within that range. You'll often see this information presented on a graph as a *frequency response curve.*

But microphones add a twist to the frequency response issue not found with other types of equipment: The frequency response of a mic varies with the spatial location of the sound source relative to the front of the mic capsule. For example, as you move around to the side of a mic, you may find that high-frequency response is diminished. Because of this, the frequency response of mics is often presented using a polar graph, which looks a bit like a map of the Earth viewed from high above the North Pole. The result is called the mic's *polar response curve.* The polar response curve documents in detail how the mic responds to various frequencies arriving from different directions. The *polar pattern* of the mic (omni, cardioid, hypercardioid, etc.) is a more general description derived from the polar response

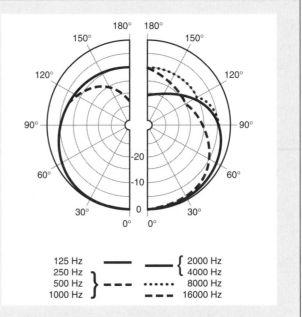

125 Hz	———	⎰ 2000 Hz
250 Hz		⎱ 4000 Hz
500 Hz	– – –	········ 8000 Hz
1000 Hz		– – 16000 Hz

curve. It's used to more practically describe how the microphone responds overall to sound coming from various directions.

When looking at a polar response graph (see accompanying graph above), 0 degrees is the front of the mic. The 0, –10, and –20 values refer to the drop in sensitivity to sound (measured in decibels; as the curve gets closer to the center of the graph, the mic gets less sensitive).

While they don't always hold true, certain generalizations can be made about dynamic and condenser mics: Dynamic mics tend to be more rugged than condensers. Dynamic mics are generally less expensive than condensers. Condensers tend to be more sensitive and tend to sound more detailed than dynamics.

Two other microphone types bear mentioning here: ribbon and boundary. *Ribbon mics* use a thin strip or ribbon of metal suspended in a magnetic field; they're related to dynamic mics. While ribbon mics can sound great, they tend to be more fragile than dynamic or condenser mics. They're not often seen outside of the confines of the recording studio.

Boundary mics, also known as "PZM" (Pressure Zone Microphone)—although this is a trademark of mic manufacturer Crown International, not a generic term—use a small mic element mounted to a flat plate. Sound is collected by the plate and reflected into the mic element. Placing the mic against a surface (or boundary) such as a wall or the floor greatly increases the mic's response. These are the small, flat mics you'll see on the stage at the theater for picking up actors' voices. They can be useful when it's impossible to use a regular mic to capture sound, but they don't tend to be very directional (see below).

Polar Patterns

Microphones can be further subdivided by how directional they are—how well they pick up sound from various directions. A mic's *polar pattern* is a description of its directionality. There are five common polar patterns and an assortment of variations. Some microphones offer one fixed polar pattern; others are capable of switching between two or more polar patterns. In general, a mic with switchable polar patterns is more versatile and flexible than a mic with one fixed pattern. An important thing to note: A directional microphone also rejects sound coming from certain directions; this can help prevent unwanted background noise from getting into the mic.

The most basic polar pattern is *omnidirectional*. As the name implies, an omnidirectional (a.k.a., "omni") mic picks up sound equally from all directions. Its polar pattern resembles a sphere. Omni mics are not good for isolating desirable sounds from background noise, but they're great for capturing all the sound that's happening in a room.

A *cardioid* mic picks up sound well from directly in front, less well from the sides, and not at all from directly behind the mic. Its polar pattern is roughly heart-shaped. Cardioid mics are by far the most common type used in recording studio applications.

A *hypercardioid* or *supercardioid* mic has a tighter polar pattern than a cardioid mic, with less sound pickup on the sides, but a bit more directly behind the mic.

Bidirectional mics, also known as *Figure 8* mics, pick up sound well from directly in front and directly behind, but not to the side—the polar pattern resembles a three-dimensional figure 8. Bidirectional microphones work well if you need to record two sound sources at once. An application might be recording an interviewer and interviewee simultaneously with one mic.

Shotgun mics take the hypercardioid polar pattern and stretch the front pickup area (known as a "lobe") *way* out. This makes them extremely directional, and useful for zeroing in on a sound source that's some distance away and surrounded by background noise. Typically you won't find shotguns used in studio situations; you'll see them being used more for broadcast and other special applications.

Other Microphone Characteristics

A variety of other microphone characteristics must be considered when choosing the right mic for a particular application. *Sensitivity* is a measure of how much electric cur-

Tube Mic Mania

Even without all the "vintage" mystique, there's something cool about tube microphones. They tend to be solid-feeling, massive (by microphone standards, anyway) objects that exude an aura of quality and craftsmanship. I have to admit, of all the types of computer, audio, and music equipment I work with, tube mics are among my favorites—they're just so *cool.*

In addition to their cool factor, tube microphones are often prized by recording engineers for the way they sound. Unlike many non-tube mics, which are designed to be neutral-sounding, tube mics are intended to add warmth, fatness, and timbral coloration to the audio they capture. Many engineers feel that tube mics also influence the dynamics of the audio they record. At low levels, this might translate to a more dynamic recording. At higher levels, tubes can add a soft compression and a subtle, pleasant distortion to the signal. No one suggests that tube mics should replace non-tube mics; rather, the idea is to add more options to your sonic palette—the best situation is to have a selection of tube and non-tube mics to choose from for each sound source.

Fortunately there's been a burst of activity on the affordable tube mic front recently. Here are some tips for getting the most out of tube microphones.

Tube Mic Tips

- Be careful! Tubes are fragile glass bottles. They're subject to damage if they, or the piece of gear they're installed in, are dropped.

- Tubes like those used in microphones and mic preamplifiers rarely need to be changed. If you do find yourself changing the tubes in your gear, be sure that you use the recommended replacement; circuits are specifically designed and tuned for particular tubes. Using the wrong model could adversely affect the sound of your equipment.

- All tubes are not created equal! Check with the manufacturer of your gear as to the best replacement.

- Tubes must warm up. Most tube mic manufacturers recommend allowing the tubes in their mics to warm up for at least 15 minutes. I prefer to let them warm up for even longer: 30 minutes, or an hour if possible.

- All tube mics that I'm aware of require an external, proprietary power supply; they won't run off of regular phantom power sources. While you probably won't damage anything by leaving the phantom power in your mixer or mic preamp turned on when using a tube mic, some manufacturers say that you may experience a slight increase in self-noise levels when phantom power is active.

- As mentioned above, all tube mics require a power supply. The mics are usually connected to the power supply with a multi-pin cable. If that cable goes bad, you're out of luck. Consider getting a spare just in case.

rent a mic generates for a given volume level. A more sensitive mic can capture quieter sounds, but may overload or distort when confronting a loud sound source. Some mics feature a built-in *pad*, which can be switched on to reduce their sensitivity.

Frequency response is a measure of how well a microphone responds to the various frequencies that make up the audio spectrum—is the mic as sensitive to bass sounds as it is to treble sounds? Will it be relatively bright sounding or dull sounding? Some mics, such as those commonly used by singers, have a bump in their midrange frequencies to help the voice be heard through a band or orchestra. A variety of factors can influence frequency response. One is diaphragm size. There are two common sizes: small diaphragm and large diaphragm. *Small diaphragm* designs are usually found in "pencil"-type mics, *large diaphragms* are found in larger, bulkier microphones. Due to their physical size, small diaphragms tend to respond better to high frequencies and to have better "detail." Large diaphragms tend to be fatter sounding and better at capturing lower frequencies. But these are generalizations; a large-diaphragm mic may have excellent detail, while a certain small-diaphragm design may be great for low frequencies. Mic manufacturers always include frequency response specifications with their mics.

Some mics offer built-in, switchable "filters" for tailoring their frequency response. The most common filter, the *low-cut filter*, can be used to reduce very low bass frequencies. This can help reduce rumble and thumps often carried into the mic by its mic stand.

Another microphone characteristic, proximity effect, is found only in non-omnidirectional mics. *Proximity effect* is the tendency of directional mics to produce more bass as they're placed closer to a sound source. Proximity effect is why announcers love to "eat" the mic; when they're right on the mic, the sound is bassier, fuller, and richer. But in many other applications, proximity effect can result in an unnatural or even a distorted sound. By moving the mic slightly farther away from the sound source, proximity effect will be reduced. A distance of a foot or so from the sound source will eliminate proximity effect from most mics.

Mic It Up!

A basic understanding of microphones is vital to capturing quality audio. By considering the microphone type, polar pattern, and other characteristics, the right mic can be chosen and accurately matched to each application. Now that you understand the basics, start putting your newfound knowledge to work—better sound will be the result!

improving your studio's acoustics

BY ROB MCGAUGHEY

Sound waves follow the basic rules of geometry (or billiards). When a sound wave hits a wall, it reflects like a cue ball striking a rail. As the cue ball travels it loses energy with distance. Each time the ball strikes a rail, it loses even more energy. This is exactly what happens with sound waves. When a sound wave hits a wall, it reflects off the surface. The amount of energy lost when a sound wave hits a wall is a function of the composition of the wall: Glass absorbs less energy (and therefore reflects more) than a carpeted surface or a ceiling tile. One way to reduce the level of reflections is with absorptive material (acoustic foam, carpet, ceiling tiles, and so on). Another method is to use diffusors. Let's take a look at some of the things that can affect the sound of a room, and what you can do to improve it.

Problem: Your control room is really a second bedroom and everything you mix sounds completely different when you listen to it in your car, on your home stereo, and elsewhere. You don't feel you can trust your ears when mixing, and it's driving you completely nuts.

Solution: Treat your mixing environment so that what comes out of your speakers isn't radically changed before it gets to your ears. You need to control sonic reflections to maximize audio integrity.

The Room

- Think about where to place the speakers within the room. You'll want to make sure that the space directly behind and to the side of each speaker is a mirror image of that of the other speaker. You don't want to have a window behind your left speaker and a solid wall behind your right speaker, or a closet with wimpy sliding doors on the right wall next to your right speaker and a solid wall on the left side. The immediate environment the speaker works in makes a big difference to its sound. Make sure both speakers are working in similar environments for maximum accuracy.

Diffusors

What are diffusors? A diffusor is a device that, when hit by a sound wave, reflects the sound more or less equally in all directions (see Figure 1). This means the level of sound wave reflections in any one direction is substantially reduced along with any acoustic anomalies that might occur.

What are diffusors used for? Diffusors are used to control acoustic energy and remove anomalies such as standing waves, slapback, echoes and fluttering, and to reduce acoustic distortion. They will widen the sweet spot in a control room and provide more consistent sound quality throughout the room.

Where do I put diffusors? Diffusors are often found along the back wall of a control room opposite the speakers. In this location, they break up direct sound waves and reduce slapback off the back wall. They can also be placed toward the rear of the room along the side walls, to remove problems such as standing waves, fluttering, and echo. Diffusors can also be used along the front wall or on the ceiling to reduce early reflections from the sound source, although more commonly you'll find absorption used in this area.

When do I use diffusors versus absorptive material (*i.e.*, acoustic foam)? A broadband absorptive material is most effective at removing the first reflections from the side walls and/or ceiling. Diffusors are better in the rear half of the room to control the acoustic energy bouncing around there. Some acousticians prefer to put diffusors behind the speakers (in the front of the room) when they're trying to control reflections without deadening the room.

Keep in mind that absorptive material will tend to make a room feel smaller, while diffusors will tend to make it feel bigger. This is especially true in small control rooms, recording rooms, and isolation booths. If you have a small recording room that requires some absorptive material to reduce reflections or fluttering, try also adding diffusors on the ceiling. The psychoacoustic effect of adding diffusors will trick your brain into thinking the room is larger than it actually is. This may make the room more comfortable to work in.

The goal is to create an acoustically accurate envi-ronment to work in. To accomplish this goal you will likely need a combination of absorptive material, diffusors, and possibly bass traps—along with a good strategy for placement of speakers, microphones, and the sources you are recording.

Will diffusors affect low frequencies? No. Most diffusors have little effect on low-frequency sound waves. In order to control the amplification of low-frequency information by the room, you need bass traps, which come in many varieties and shapes. (Standard 1-, 2-, or 3-inch-thick sheets of acoustic foam also have little effect on low frequencies. However, there are some considerably thicker foam materials that can function as bass traps.)

Are there cost-effective alternatives to the commercially available diffusors? Yes and no. The best and most effective diffusors are those from reputable acoustics companies who have developed products based on proven acoustic principles and tested them to ensure that they deliver what they promise. However, there are other less expensive and more practical things that may function as diffusors in the real world. In a small control room, try placing a bookshelf or two along the back wall opposite the speakers. Fill the bookshelves with books of various sizes—owner's manuals, technical specifications, back issues of magazines, etc. Try to break up the flat areas. An idea that's worked for me is to hang my various coiled cables along the wall. Another option is non-flat art or decorative items hung on the wall. Remember to make sure that none of these "treatments" resonates when the volume is turned up, or you'll drive yourself nuts trying to find the source of the vibration and ringing you hear!

Think of diffusors and other acoustic treatments as tools to help improve the sound quality of your recordings—they can affect the quality of the finished product as much as any other piece of gear in your studio. You'll find that by adding some acoustic treatments, moving things around in your room, and taking advantage of its shape/features, you'll create a better sonic environment to work in. Understanding the fundamentals of acoustics and a little experimentation to determine how, when, and where to use various tools should prove invaluable.

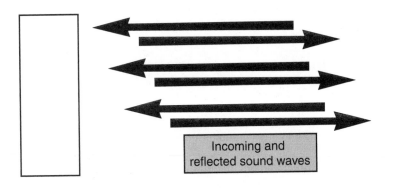

Figure 1 A bare wall or other hard surface will simply reflect sound waves back into the room, causing possible acoustic problems.

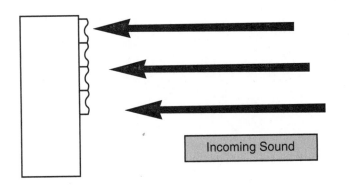

Figure 2 With a material such as acoustic foam installed, sound is absorbed rather than reflected. While this can cut down on acoustic problems, it can also make a room seem "small" and uncomfortably dead-sounding.

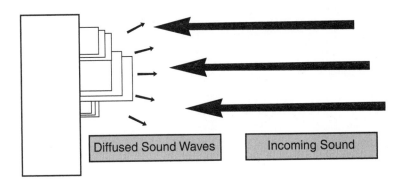

Figure 3 Acoustic energy is reflected off of a diffusor in many directions, breaking up direct reflections back into the room. This can make the room feel larger and more comfortable.

• Another variable is the distance between your speakers and the room's walls. The best distance depends on the speaker design. Many speaker manufacturers include information on optimum speaker placement; dig this out and read it. Generally, for smaller, nearfield-style designs, you'll want the speakers at least 18 inches from any nearby walls, placed in front of you so they form an equilateral (equal-sided) triangle between the two speakers and your ears. The distance between your speakers and the walls will dramatically affect bass response.

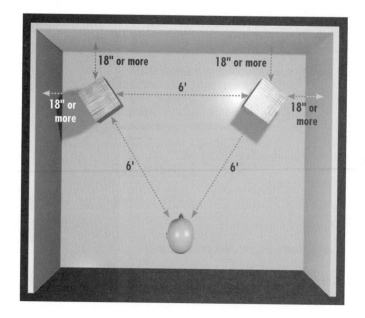

Figure 4 In general, speakers should be placed away from walls and corners. The two speakers should form an equilateral triangle with the listener's head.

- You need to be aware of the sound coming out of each speaker and the amount of time that will pass before that sound will hit a hard surface and bounce back to the listening position. The reflections with the shortest time delay (first reflections) are the most offensive and will require acoustic treatment.

Controlling First Reflections

1. Sit down in a chair in the mix position facing the speakers. Your head and the speakers should form an equilateral triangle, as described above.

2. Get a small mirror and have a friend hold the mirror against the wall at ear level on your right side. Have them move the mirror along the wall until you can look out of the corner of your eye and see the tweeter of your speaker reflected in the mirror. Mark this spot on the wall, as it's an area that will require treatment. Repeat this step for your left side.

3. Now that you've marked the first reflection spots on your right and left sides, look around and see if there are additional hard surfaces that will cause reflections that are roughly the same distance away from your head as the spots you just marked. You may find trouble areas on the ceiling, floor, mixing console, computer desk, gear racks, computer monitor, etc. Use the same mirror technique to identify these other trouble areas. Some of these areas, such as the surface of the mixing console, furniture, or computer monitor, may be difficult to

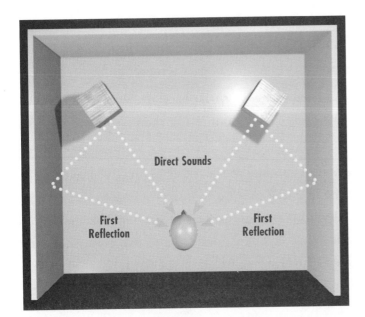

Figure 5 First reflections are a major concern when setting up a mixing position. The slightly delayed arrival of reflected sound can wreak havoc on sonic accuracy.

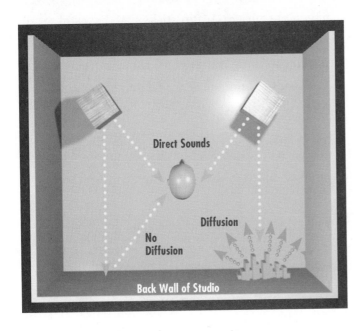

Figure 6 Unless there is some sort of diffuser on the back wall of the studio, reflections of the speaker's sound will come directly back to the listener. By breaking up the reflections, the sonic accuracy of the room can be improved.

treat. Our goal is to reduce as many as we can. If you can't treat a spot, try moving or changing the angle of the offending item.

The Treatment

1. Place absorbent acoustic material on the spots that you identified in the previous section. You'll want to have at least a 2 feet x 4 feet of coverage, and you may want to increase coverage to 4 x 4 feet on each side. If you've identified areas on the ceiling, you may want to apply treatment there as well. You can use acoustic

foam, heavy curtains, or other treatments. To increase the absorption of acoustic foam, leave approximately one inch of air space between the foam and the wall. This can be done by using spacers behind the foam when mounting it.

Another option is to mount angled reflective surfaces on the wall such that the first reflections are sent to the back of the room rather than coming straight to the listener.

2. Place diffusers along the back wall opposite the speakers to prevent direct reflections from coming back to the listening area. A poor man's method of diffusion is to place bookshelves filled with books and objects of varying sizes and other furniture along the back wall. While this may not be as effective as buying manufactured diffusers, it will help. The idea is to break up the flat surfaces along the back wall and decrease the sound pressure level of the reflections bouncing back into the mixing area.

3. Clap your hands, snap your fingers, or hit two drum sticks together, and listen. If you hear a fluttering type of echo in the room, ringing, or standing waves (where a particular frequency seems to jump out at you), try to figure out what location it's coming from. These acoustic anomalies are caused by sound waves bouncing back and forth between two reflective surfaces (*e.g.*, parallel flat walls), so start moving around the room as you make noise until you can isolate the problem area. You can reduce these acoustic aberrations by placing something in their path, such as acoustic material, diffusers, wall hangings, or furniture.

Controlling Bass Frequencies

The previous steps will not have much effect on bass frequencies. Here's some suggestions for dealing with low-end problems:

1. Move your speakers away from walls and especially corners. Make sure the distance between each speaker and the nearest corner is the same. Walls amplify bass frequencies; when two walls meet in a corner the amplification is doubled, and when two walls and a floor or ceiling meet the amplification is quadrupled.

2. Fill the corners of your room with something. One solution is to buy bass traps and install them. There are a number of different types of bass traps and they have a wide range of cost and effectiveness. The best bass traps I've found are those by RPG Acoustics. More cost-effective are the foam cornerfills from Auralex Acoustics, which can be used to line your room's corners. The idea is to remove the corners of the room from the acoustic equation—fill them with something.

Conclusions

Control room acoustics and treatment is a deep and complex subject. These suggestions should help you improve your mixes with only a modest investment in acoustic materials and time. My advice is to think, listen, and experiment. Get opinions from other people and use audio material you are very familiar with in listening tests. Be aware that what sounds the most pleasing may not necessarily be the most accurate. Also note that it's possible to overdo acoustic treatment; a completely dead room (too much absorption) will feel very uncomfortable to work in, one with too much bass treatment will result in unbalanced mixes, and so on.

After each change you make to your room, remix a familiar project and listen to it in other environments; compare it to your old mix and to similar commercial mixes you admire. Improving control room sonics can be a long process, but the reward is hearing your mixes sounding great wherever they're played. It's definitely worth the effort!

working efficiently

Waste less time, make more music

BY MITCH GALLAGHER

few of us have as much time as we'd prefer to devote to our music. With jobs, family, day-to-day chores, and luxuries such as sleep, making music ends up lower on the list than we'd like. It makes sense, then, to put what music-making time you have to good use by working as efficiently as possible. If you save even ten minutes each time you fire up your rig, you've done yourself a big favor!

Here are some tips that will streamline the process of working in your studio, and will help you get the most from your music-making time.

Maintenance

There's nothing worse than trying to be creative using gear that's not operating at its best. In commercial studios, there's a tech who comes in during down time and makes sure everything is working well. Most of us would love to have such a person visiting our home/project studios, but the reality is that we'll probably be doing it ourselves. I've found that things run more smoothly if I occasionally schedule an afternoon to maintain my rig. This includes getting gear repaired, cleaning up, fixing or replacing bad cables, rearranging racks, backing up and documenting sessions, filing CDs and disks, upgrading software, maintaining my hard drives, or whatever. If I don't do this, I end up interrupting sessions to take care of such tasks, which is sure to kill the creative flow.

Signal Routing

Take a look at how your rig is cabled together. Do you find you're crawling behind racks to change routings? If so, consider routing your gear through patchbays. A patchbay brings all the connectors out from the back panels of your equipment to a central location. Using short jumper cables you can then easily connect the gear in whatever manner is necessary for the current task.

This may not be the ideal situation, though. At one point, I had seven patchbays that brought every connection in my rig out to a central point. While this was flexible, it also meant that my signals ran through twice as much cable length (one cable going to the patchbay and another running back to wherever the item was connected). I invariably found that at least one of those multitudinous connections was loose, intermittent, or noisy at any given time—just keeping everything working was a hassle. I realized that despite having all those bays, I rarely ended up changing the routing much. Over time, I did away with the bays and settled into a much simpler hardwired setup that covers me 98% of the time and has far fewer cable/connection problems.

Whichever method you use, wire up your rig in the way you use it the most often. If you have to insert a patch cable into a bay or crawl behind your gear very often, things are likely not routed as well as they could be. If you do use patchbays or change the routing of your studio, be sure to document what you're doing—you'll want that information if you need to recreate a routing or setup.

Have Instruments Set Up and Ready to Go

There's nothing worse than having inspiration strike, then losing it while you fool around getting a mic set up, or your guitar rig plugged in. I keep a mic plugged into my mixer and ready to go at all times. No, I'm not suggesting you leave your $5,000 tube mic sitting out. In my case, I have an old mic that's survived years of onstage abuse; it's not the highest-fidelity mic I own, but if I get a song idea, it will capture things well enough for me to document the idea. It's always plugged into a mixer channel and routed into my recorder for immediate use. Some musicians like to keep a small cassette recorder with a built-in mic at hand for the same purpose—just hit record and you're ready to go without having to power up your whole rig.

Likewise, acoustic, electric, and bass guitars are on stands easily at hand. There's a cable hanging right beside them ready to be plugged into whichever one I want to use. The other end of the cable stays plugged into a direct box and is routed into a mixer channel and on to my recorder. I won't claim to capture the perfect tone with this rig. The idea is to be able to get ideas down with a minimum of hassle and time.

Use Sound Templates

I have a number of synths and samplers in my rig, which is great—there's certainly a broad palette of sonic colors there from which to choose. Unfortunately, getting them all loaded with sounds, finding the patches I want, setting up MIDI channels, and routing them all through the mixer can take some time. To speed things when I want to compose, I've set up my Kurzweil K2500 with an autoload bank of useful sounds. When I power up my studio, the K2500 automatically loads the sounds I've specified into RAM. I always leave it connected to my MIDI interface and mixer so it's immediately ready to go.

The patches I've selected probably won't be the final sounds that make it into a mix, but I've put together a selection that covers most of the bases I need for basic composition: piano, strings, bass, synth lead, pads, drums, and so on. Once I've got my ideas in my sequencer, it's much easier (and less of an intrusion on the initial creative moment) to go back and replace the default sounds with specific sounds from other synths and samplers, or to program sounds that are perfect for the parts I've created. You could use a General MIDI-compatible module or bank in a similar way. The key is to limit yourself to a "writer's bank" so that you can easily jump to the piano or strings you use for composing without having to scroll through lists and banks of patches to find the one you want. You might also consider using the same MIDI channels for particular instruments—piano is always on channel one, strings are always channel three, and so on.

Software Templates

It's hard to know exactly how many tracks you'll need for a song in your sequencer or digital audio program, but you can set things up in advance that will help you get started. I keep a template song ready to go for my sequencer that has MIDI tracks pre-assigned to the K2500 bank I mentioned above, a click track playing, and so on. When I want to sequence, I open the template song, record-arm a track, and I'm ready to go.

Similarly, in my audio software template, I have several tracks set up to record from my mixer (including channels for the mic and guitar direct box mentioned above). I also have aux sends and returns set up to address my external hardware effects. All I have to do is start the program, load my template, and I'm recording—with effects, if I so desire.

On the Mac, consider saving your templates as Stationary Pad documents. (On your hard drive, select your template file by clicking it once. Choose "Get Info" from the "File" menu. When the information window opens, select the "Stationary Pad" box on the lower right, then close the window.) Saving as stationary creates a file type that can be modified as usual. But when you go to save the file, the program you're using will prevent you from overwriting the old file—you'll be forced to give the file a new name. This prevents you from accidentally saving over your template file in the heat of battle.

Having templates for my various programs has made me much more efficient. I have both 16- and 24-bit audio templates, sequencer templates that address certain synths, notation program templates that cover the various ensembles I compose for, and so on.

Become a Power User

Watching most people operate their computers drives me up the wall. It seems as if they're working in the slowest way possible—using the mouse, trackball, or track-pad. In some cases, that's the only way to do things. But virtually every piece of software available has at least *some* key equivalents for oft-used commands and short cuts for accomplishing common tasks. Put these to work and you'll find yourself becoming much more efficient. Take a moment and dig out the listing of the key equivalents for your sequencer and audio software. Spend some time getting acquainted with how much you can do without ever taking your hands off the keyboard. Plus, many sequencer programs include MIDI equivalents for various commands; you can create much of your sequence without ever having to pull your fingers off your controller's keys.

It can be difficult to get used to using key equivalents if you're a long-time mouser. The only solution I can offer is to force yourself to work without the mouse. Put it in an inaccessible place, put your list of key equivalents by your keyboard, and resolve to use them wherever possible. When I tried this myself, I found that my productivity soared, particularly when I was performing repetitive tasks.

Keep Things You Need Close at Hand

Few things annoy me more than having to stop the creative process to find a disk, locate a cable, or find a formatted tape. Organize your studio so that the accessories and media you need are easily at hand. One way to do this is to install rack drawers and shelves into your equipment racks. I've done so, and found that these are perfect for holding DAT tapes, blank CD-Rs, guitar tuners, and other things I need on a regular basis. A set of shelves or a file cabinet in your studio may serve the same purpose for you.

Ergonomics

Finally, take a look at your studio's layout. Are you always getting on the floor to program patches on a certain synth module? Maybe it would be better to locate it higher up in a rack. Is your mixer easily accessible, or do you have to get up and walk across the room to turn up a channel? Experiment with different layouts, and don't be afraid to try things and refine the rig as you go—this is often time well spent. Just don't stop a session to do it; schedule another time to tear things apart.

Working efficiently can be a difficult thing when you're simultaneously wearing the hats of composer, musician, recording engineer, producer, maintenance tech, and studio gofer. If you spend a few minutes making sure things are working well, the tools and items you need are at hand, and that you've pre-set up as much as possible, you'll find your productivity has improved. Ultimately, this translates to more time for you to spend making music—and isn't that what it's all about?

combating silence

The easy way to troubleshoot studio problems

BY MITCH GALLAGHER

modern audio gear is simply amazing. The affordable power we have available to us for creating, manipulating, and recording music has reached near to the point of miraculous. Much of the time the technology behind all that power works very well—surprisingly so. But on those occasions when there are problems with the technology, solving them can be an onerous and frustrating task, even for those with a lot of experience. My advice: The next time you run into a snag with your rig, take a deep breath, step back, and call someone else to solve it for you.

Not possible? Okay, you're stuck doing the job yourself. Go ahead and take that deep breath, then carefully proceed. I've found that troubleshooting is usually easiest if you take a logical approach to it, rather than trying one random thing after another. Adhering to the following guidelines has made the process much less painful for me.

1. **Vent.** It's tough to take a studied, logical approach to a problem if you're not calm. There are many approaches to calming down after a gear snag, including the Computer Monitor Toss, the MIDI Cable Strangle, and the Mixing Console Flip. I prefer the Vocal Expostulation Method, which is closely related to Primal Scream Therapy. This method involves high-volume, detail-oriented descriptions of the problem item, its ancestry, and its mating habits. Be sure small children, pets, and other sensitive ears have left the vicinity before using this technique.

2. **Check the volume!** The first thing we do when our gear doesn't work is crank up the volume, trying to force the sound out of the speakers. Then, when we go back and plug or unplug cables, or when we finally get things working, we're greeted with blasting levels, feedback, headphone-pierced ears, or blown speakers. Always verify the volume is set to a reasonable level before you begin to troubleshoot.

The First Things to Check

While it's possible for just about anything to go wrong with a system, most problems can be traced to one of just a few common sources. I always check these items first before assuming the problem lies deeper in the system.

Audio Hardware

1. Pilot Error. A huge percentage of problems can be traced to this source. Whether it's due to owner's manual avoidance, incorrect connections, or just a switch in the wrong position, pilot error is a primary suspect.

2. Cables. Right behind pilot error is cabling. Broken solder joints, pinched shielding, just plain orneriness, cables are out to get you. Always verify (twice) that the "good" cable you're using for testing is indeed good—and don't rule out the possibility that more than one cable has self-destructed.

3. Cables. After I've checked all the possible cables (and some of the impossible ones) I proceed to check all the possible cables (and some of the impossible ones). Cables are sly beasts, and they'll purposefully be intermittent just to annoy you.

4. Connections. I wish I had a ten-dollar bill for every time I've discovered a problem was due to a cable coming partially unplugged, a corroded connector, or a worn-out patchbay jack.

Computers

1. System level software conflicts. On the Mac, it's extensions and control panels; on the PC, it's drivers, IRQs, and DMAs. Whichever platform you're working on, take note of when the problem arises. If it's during startup or when rebooting, odds are something at the system level is at fault. Reboot with a minimal or clean system and start adding things back in until the problem returns.

2. Cables. As with audio cables, computer cables are the root of many an evil. Verify and re-verify that all yours are good before looking for other problems. Many types of computer cable chains can be run only for limited distances before they get unstable. Try rebuilding the chain with the shortest cables you can.

3. Connections. Unless they're screwed down tight (and even if they are), computer connections can work free and cause intermittent behavior, or make the computer behave in a strange fashion. It's also easy to bend the pins in some multi-pin computer plugs, which results in hard-to-trace symptoms.

4. Termination. Many computer peripherals need to be properly terminated to function correctly. Older SCSI devices and some samplers, in particular, can be cantankerous. (Don't assume anything: I once had a SCSI chain that required two terminators to function: one in the middle and one at the end.)

3. **Fly solo.** If you're working with someone else, it's conceivable that they'll want to help with the troubleshooting process. While an offer of assistance is always appreciated, it's often better to go it alone. For me, there have been too many occasions where I'm checking one connection, convinced it's the problem, only to find later that my "helper" had pulled some other cable or made a change to the system without my knowledge.

4. **Examine the patient.** Once you've vented and established who is doing the troubleshooting, take a moment to think about the problem. Is there no sound?

A Real-life Scenario

You get home from work. You're all excited to get into your studio to try out a new chord progression that's been banging away in your head all day. You power your rig up, sit down in front of your favorite keyboard, put your foot on the sustain pedal, begin playing your new masterpiece, and ... the silence is deafening. What to do? (Aside from throwing a screaming fit.)

Start by thinking about what's going on, and streamline the troubleshooting process by making some educated guesses. For example: Since no sound is coming out of any of the speakers, the problem probably lies before the speaker stage. More likely it's something earlier in the chain. Similarly, since nothing is coming out of either the left or right sides of the sound system, it's likely that some piece of gear is at fault, rather than a cable, which would probably affect only one side of the stereo field or the other. Making note of facts like this can help you decide where to start your troubleshooting efforts. Once you've decided how to begin, there are a number of ways to proceed. Let's say you've got a synth keyboard plugged into two channels on a mixer, which then feeds into a set of powered monitors. Here's one possible trouble-shooting path:

1. Verify that power is reaching all components.
2. Verify that all components are hooked up correctly.
3. Plug a set of headphones into the keyboard and determine if the unit is making sound on its own. If so, use it as a sound source to continue checking. If not, you may have found your problem. Verify that the keyboard's output cabling works properly.
4. Using the verified keyboard, check that sound is getting into the mixer. Look at the mixer's meters and indicators, and listen with the headphones plugged into the mixer's headphone output. Verify the mixer's cabling.
5. Verify that the mixer's routing is set up properly.
6. Re-verify that the mixer routing is set properly!
7. Try plugging the keyboard into another channel on the mixer.
8. If you are unable to verify whether sound is getting into and/or out of the mixer, you may have found your problem. Patch the keyboard straight into the monitor system using a known good cable—but be very, very careful of volume levels when doing this.
9. Patch the keyboard back into the mixer. Verify that the cables coming out of the mixer and into the monitor system are good.

Proceed through the system in this fashion, patching around each component and verifying its cabling until you determine where the problem lies.

Is there a hum? If so, does it sound like a ground loop or an open connection? Computer crash? When is it occurring? During startup, when you perform certain edits, or when you access a particular hard drive? Clearly define what the symptoms are, so you know what to look for.

5. **Diagnose the illness.** Once you know what the symptoms are, think about what might be a possible cause. Make a list of possible things to check. For example, if you're not getting any sound from your system: Is the source you think is playing a sound actually playing that sound? Is AC power getting to everything?

Have any power/audio/MIDI/data cables come partially unplugged? Have any cables spontaneously self-destructed? Is the mixer routing correct, and so on?

6. **Put it back.** Most problems with a system occur when something new is added. Knowing this, it's a good idea to verify that your system works before you add something new. That way, if there's a problem after the addition, you can remove it, put the system back to the way it was before the change, and have a firm baseline to work from. If you're making multiple changes to the rig, never add or change more than one thing at a time. Always check to make sure that the system works after each new addition. When rewiring or setting up a system for the first time, periodically stop and verify that it's working up to that point.

7. **Start from one end.** If you're trying to trace a problem, it generally works best to start at one end of the chain and to work forward or backward from there. I usually start at the beginning (the source of whatever audio is playing), and establish at what point the signal is not getting through to later stages in the chain. For this reason, I prefer gear that has metering or signal-present indicators, as well as gear that has its own headphone jack. As you're working your way through the chain, eliminate any possible variables at each stage: bad cables, incorrect routings, active mute or solo switches—troubleshooting is really just a glorified process of elimination combined with a little educated guessing.

8. **One step at a time.** As you're troubleshooting a system, never skip a component, cable, or gain stage or assume that it works okay. Even if you're seeing meter action, verify that audio is actually exiting the item. A little-known addendum to Murphy's Law states that the one step or item you skip while troubleshooting is sure to be the one that's causing the difficulty.

make music now!

recording a song in seven easy steps

Getting your music projects from here to there

BY JIM BORDNER

You probably know the feeling. No matter how hard you work or how good your ideas, you just can't seem to get them down in a finished form. Maybe you've got a hard drive or tape full of bits and pieces, but none of them is developed the way you'd like. Or maybe your hard drive or tape is bare, because you just can't get a handle on where to begin.

I know the feeling, too. I write and produce commercial music, cranking out tunes from thin air to CD master against tight deadlines and with minimal direction. Yes, I have a lot of cool tools to do it with. But cool tools don't make music on their own. It wasn't all that long ago that I was teaching myself the basics of MIDI production with a keyboard, a plastic computer, and a single General MIDI module. I produced my first paying jobs on that rig. The lessons I learned then are the same ones that get the engine cranked over in my business today.

The primary lesson is this: You get your best results when you have a plan and follow it. As the motivational guys say, "Plan your work and work your plan." As corny as it sounds, that's exactly how things get done.

Did I hear someone say, "Oh, how can you put a stiff, regimented process on something as free-flowing and mysterious as creating art?" Well, you have to, or you'll never get the music down so others can hear it. You can play for your own amusement forever, if you choose, and that's unarguably a creative act. But as one of the rapidly growing number of artist/engineers, you've chosen an art form that takes a lot of knowledge and a lot of work in all the disciplines that affect your art. Composition and songwriting, musicianship, production, and engineering are all very different, and you need to develop skills in all of them. It can be a bit daunting, making the distance between today and the day you finish your *magnum opus* look like 100 miles of undiscovered country.

In this chapter I'll give you a guided tour of the landscape. Once you know your way around, you'll feel bolder and more prepared to explore on your own. Remember that the specific approach I'm giving you here is just a guideline. There are as many different ways through the musical wilderness as there are musicians, and no one way is best or right; there's only what's best or right for you.

If you're having trouble getting your projects to the end of the trail, try following this step-by-step procedure.

1. Choose your material. If you're paying a commercial studio to help you create your songs, you can pretty much expect that they'll have the tools and talent necessary to make your musical vision into reality. But when you're an artist/engineer working in your own studio, you sometimes have to make decisions based on what your gear is capable of. So material selection is important. If you don't play guitar and your studio is MIDI-only, a flat-out heavy-metal raver is probably out. Likewise, if your synthesizers have limited polyphony, you might want to wait before trying that full orchestral piece with the dueling pianos.

If it's original material, make sure you've really finished writing it. Sit down and play a solo version of the tune all the way through. Do it several times. Does it flow nicely from beginning to end and feel satisfying when you're done, or is there a bump in the road or a clunky passage? If the latter, keep working until you enjoy playing the piece from beginning to end. If you don't like playing it, nobody's going to like hearing it.

If it's someone else's music, spend some time getting to know the tune intimately. Improvise on it, make interesting mistakes, and listen hard to the chord changes, paying special attention to moving lines and countermelodies that you find in the chords. A solid knowledge of the tune's "skeleton" will be very important in the next few steps.

Now you've got the tune under your skin. Let's move on to arranging.

2. Create a scratch arrangement. How you approach the arrangement depends on your level of musical knowledge and your own preference. Maybe you like to write things out on staff paper so you can see how the parts interact. Maybe you just sit down and jam, freezing bits of improv into a cool confection. No matter how you approach it, arranging your piece will make the following steps a bit easier and more successful. This is because the arranging stage gives you a chance to make some decisions in advance, and fit the instrumentation to both your skills as a player and your capabilities as an engineer.

For example, tracking will go much easier if you have a clear understanding of what each instrument in your virtual band is supposed to be doing. If you have decided in advance that the role of the piano is primarily to accent the hi-hat with upper-register chords, you'll spend less of your tracking time experimenting with piano lines and more time getting the part in the pocket.

Far too often we skip this stage and start tracking parts as soon as we have the musical idea. We spend hours upon hours playing with every patch in our synths, trying this, layering that. If something cool happens, we keep the part. And what we end up with is too many instruments playing too many things. The finished piece may have its moments, but they're far outweighed by a lack of direction. Spending some time arranging will keep your musical ideas on track.

You don't need to have a degree in advanced theory to arrange your own material. Begin with an understanding of what kind of tune you're doing: R&B, slammin' dance track, super-pop, rock 'n' roll, whatever. Think about the instrumentation you most commonly hear in the genre, and spend some time thinking about some alternatives or interesting additions to those instruments. Then spend a little time figuring out basic parts for the instruments you've selected, letting each instrument have its say while keeping out of the way of the others.

3. Make a demo. The purpose of a demo is to give you a road map. Not a Rand McNally work of cartography, but the kind of map you'd draw on a napkin. Just slam down some rough parts to get a sense of how your arrangement works. Play your parts quickly—don't worry about mistakes and fine-tuning, just get 'em down. Give yourself three takes to nail it, and move on.

The same goes for mixing. Mix the demo fast and hot, without agonizing over effects and panning. Just get it down—with this important *caveat:* You're going to be using this version of the tune down the road in a couple of different ways, so you have to make sure it *feels* good. If it makes you smile to listen to it, you're on the right track.

The demo gives you a reference point and a foundation for refining your ideas. As you listen to it over the next couple of days, you'll find yourself thinking of better ways to approach the parts, nice harmonies or countermelodies, or cool things that could happen in percussion. You'll also get a clearer picture of the finished whole.

Now that you've spent some time with your demo, go back to your arrangement and adjust things accordingly. At this point, you're ready for the real thing: tracking.

4. Track the parts. By thinking seriously about the arrangement and spending some time making a demo, you've made a lot of decisions about the piece, and should be feeling pretty confident about what the parts should be. Now it's time to get serious about playing those parts. There are two ways you'll approach tracking, depending on whether you work alone or with other musicians.

If you're working alone, your goal will be to play each part *exactly* the way you want it (or at least close enough to make for easy editing) before moving on to the next. Because most pop music is dependent on the tight interaction of kick drum and bass guitar, I like to start tracking with the drum parts first. Planning the feel of the drum part was part of your arranging step, so all you have to do is get the part you have in your head down on tape (or in your sequencer). There's nothing wrong with using pre-recorded MIDI drum tracks (such as the collection from DrumTrax, which I have used on several jingles and video scores). A lot of those MIDI file drum parts groove nicely, and usually feature cool breaks and fills that you might not think of on your own. Once the drums are down, move on to the bass, keeping it tight with the kick drum. When you mix, you're going to want those two to sound like one instrument, so keeping them locked up is a priority. Once the bass is perfect, lay down the instruments in whatever order feels right to you. I usually track whatever carries the greatest harmonic content at this point (electric piano, rhythm guitar, whatever is playing the chords). If the song contains vocals, I'll lay them down next, and then start adding instruments that play fills or rhythmic elements (horns, Clavinet, and so on). I like to save solos for last: Soloing is always better when the whole band is jamming behind you.

If you work with other musicians, you may want to track the rhythm section together, to get a groove going. This is also another good use for your demo: Giving a copy of the demo to your players before the session gives them a chance to get the song in their bones, too.

Whether you work alone or with others, and whether the tracks are audio or MIDI, track the parts all the way through several times, keeping the best three takes or so. MIDI software and digital audio in computers have made it possible to "cut and paste" a perfect part, repeating precisely the same performance every time through a verse or chorus. But you may decide you want the human energy that slight variations in performance can lend. Maybe one of those three takes feels great all the way through because the player really found the pocket and stayed there. Or perhaps you'll decide to "comp" a perfect but still human-sounding take by combining the best phrases from all three. Either way, my best tracking experiences have come from playing the parts all the way through. Once you have a few solid performances, it's much easier to go back and punch-in minor fixes.

You'll find that when you're tracking yourself, you'll know whether the take is good or not by how it felt while you were playing. Keep in mind that the pocket can be an elusive place, and getting into it once or twice during a session may be all you're going to get. So if you know you're cooking and you throw down a big whoppin' mistake, *don't stop playing!* Just stay in the groove and jam on. You can always fix that clam in the next stage: editing.

5. Edit the parts. Whether you're working in MIDI, digital audio, or a combination of the two, your computer gives you an amazing amount of editing power. Here's how to use and not abuse it.

First solo each track and listen for really obvious goofs. These mistakes may be covered up in the mix with the whole band howling away, but you don't want them in there, so fix them now. Think of it as good housekeeping. Clean tracks make mixing easier, so just go through them one at a time and fix the clunkers.

Now start listening to instruments together in pairs or trios (bass and drums for example), and listen for places where the instruments are working well together and places where they fight or don't feel right rhythmically. There's a general rule of thumb in my studio: Try everything before you resort to quantizing! Unless you're specifically going for a machine-like feel (some forms of dance music are firmly rooted in this), don't reach for the quantization commands if you can help it. Selective quantizing can work wonders, but the only way to use it effectively is to know where the pocket is. And you learn this through experimentation and trial-and-error. If a kick drum and bass don't feel right together, for example, try moving one or the other backward or forward just a few "clicks" and listen to how it changes the feel. Experiment until it feels good to you.

When editing, keep this fact in mind: When a group of instruments play at about the same time, the first one to talk gets the emphasis. So let's say your whole band lands together on one big chord right at the first beat of measure 14, and you want to emphasize the piano. Instead of turning it up in the mix, try moving just the piano chord a couple clicks ahead, to measure 13, beat 4, click 470 (assuming your sequencer has a resolution of 480 clock pulses per quarter note). The piano will jump out of the chord.

Now that you've cleaned things up and adjusted their timing, play through a rough mix of the whole piece with all instruments playing. Listen for harmonic oddities such as clashing tones or other problems. If you're working in MIDI only and using one or two multitimbral modules to produce all your instruments, listen for note stealing. You may have to make some hard decisions at this point. That Clavinet lick may be awesome, but is it really more important than the cool bass walk-up it's stepping on? The instruments you've chosen have to share a very small space, so teach them to play nice and share.

When you've got all the tracks working well together, I advocate one more step if your recording rig allows it. Now is a good time to split out your MIDI drum kit into individual tracks by recording them separately as audio tracks, either on a multitrack recorder or as tracks in your digital audio sequencer. If you can't do this (because you don't have a multitrack machine or digital audio capability in your computer) it's not essential. But if you can, you'll have greater control over the sound of the drums and the balance between instruments in the kit when you get to the final mixing stage.

6. The final mix.   There is no way to overemphasize the importance of the mix. You may have written the sweetest song, laid down the phattest beats, ripped off the most smokin' hot solos, and your tune can still arrive D.O.A. if it has a bad case of Mixosis. Here's how to make sure this dreaded killer of good music doesn't infect your work.

To begin with, start with fresh ears. When you've finished tracking and editing, let the song sit for a day or two without listening to it. This way, when you begin mixing, you can bring some fresh excitement to the piece, instead of sitting there thinking, "Ai-yi-yi, not that chorus again, I can't stand it anymore!" To be honest, I rarely have the time for this luxury in my commercial work. You'll notice that the word "deadline" contains the word "dead," as in "dead in the water" or "you're a dead man." I frequently have no choice but to begin mixing as soon as the tracks are edited, or even while the tracks are being edited. But my best-sounding projects are the ones where I had the time to freshen my perspective on the music by walking away from it for a day.

You may have a physical mixing board, you may be mixing MIDI and audio using the virtual mixer in your sequencing software, or you may be controlling levels in a multitimbral synth with MIDI volume messages. No matter how your studio is configured, mixing requires patience and careful listening.

There are as many approaches to mixing as there are engineers, but most of us do some common things while mixing any form of pop music. Begin with all the faders down, all effects and EQ off, and your main output turned up. The rhythm is the foundation, so bring up the drums first. If you were able to track your drums separately, great. Bring up the kick, snare, and hat tracks and listen for balance. Use your pan controls to place them in the mix (keeping in mind that in most pop music, kick drum and bass are run right down the middle of the stereo field). Now add toms and cymbals, taking the same approach (these instruments tend to get panned a bit wider than the first three). Finally, bring up any incidental percussion and do the same. If you're working with a stereo drum mix coming out of a soundcard or a synth module, more than likely the drums will show up panned correctly and will hopefully be pretty well balanced.

Either way, remember that you need headroom for everything else that's coming later. Keep an eye on the stereo master meters on your mixer or on your mixdown deck (reel-to-reel, DAT, cassette, whatever). As you're getting the drums together, don't max out the levels; leave some room for other instruments.

Next I like to bring up the bass, finding a level that lets it sit nicely with the kick drum, so the two instruments sound like one. Don't reach for the EQ yet—remember that the mix will sound different with each additional instrument, so wait until you've got things in place before you decide on EQ and effects.

If your song has vocals, bring them up now, and set the level so it sounds right with the drums and bass. If you listen to most pop records with an ear toward their arranging, you'll notice that many have long passages—whole verses and choruses—that are nothing but drums, bass, and vocals. This is the backbone of a pop record, so mix these three until they sound like a pretty good song all by themselves. Next, bring in and balance any background or harmony vocals.

Now you can start adding the remaining tracks in whatever order you feel is best. I tend to mix in the same general order I track things in; at this point I bring in harmonically complex chordal instruments, setting levels and pan controls so that they don't interfere with the vocals. Then I add instruments that play fills and embellishments, and finally instrumental solos. If you're making instrumental music with a lead instrument such as sax or guitar, treat it like the lead vocal in our example scenario.

After listening carefully, start adding EQ and effects (reverb, chorus, etc). I don't have the space to get into the specifics of using EQ and effects—whole books have been written on the subject. My best advice is to try not to overdo it. A little judicious EQ on the background tracks (try cutting frequencies rather than boosting them) can help clear a path for a vocal or featured instrument, and often just a touch of reverb is better than a huge wash (again, depending on the kind of music you're mixing).

When it's sounding good to you, go ahead and record ("print") the mix to whatever medium you're using. If your mix requires manual fader moves, practice them a few times before recording the mix. If you had to make some tough decisions, try printing three or four different versions of the mix taking those decisions into account. At this point, the mix is done—but there's still one more step remaining.

7. Evaluate your work. Make a copy of the final mix on cassette or CD and play it through as many different audio systems as you can: on a boombox, in your car, and on your home stereo. Does it hold up? Is the mix clear and unmuddied? Is the vocal present and understandable? Are you happy with the balance and the groove? Does the arrangement make sense? And does it still contain the excitement of your original demo?

If you can answer yes to these questions, congratulations. You've done it. If the answer to any of these questions is "no" (or if you hear other things you're not happy with), then pinpoint the problem and go back to the place where it happened—the composition, the arrangement, the tracking, or the mixdown—and take another run at it.

The evaluation stage deserves the same attention you give any of the others, because this is where a lot of the learning happens. You can get feedback from friends and family (they may not know about music, but they know what they like). You'll also learn how to make a portable mix with your particular monitors. No monitors are perfect, and mixing well is often a matter of simply getting used to the idiosyncrasies of the speakers you use. Most important, the evaluation stage gives you a chance to step back and listen with fresh ears. Detach yourself from the process of making the music and simply listen for its merits and its flaws.

That's It!

You're now the proud creator of a finished piece of work. As you apply this process and begin discovering variations in it that work best for you, I'd like you to keep three ideas in mind:

First, pay complete attention to each stage. I'm a guy who loves good craftsmanship, and there's no better exponent of this than Norm Abrams of *The New Yankee Workshop* on PBS. Now, I'm no handyman—I grew a beard because I got tired of cutting myself shaving—but I love to watch Norm, because he embodies craftsmanship. When he's cutting a rabbet or routing an edge, he gives the cut his whole attention. No wonder when he starts gluing the pieces together, they fit to aircraft tolerances (what Norm calls "pretty good"). So when you're composing, for example, just compose, with your full attention given to melody and harmony. Don't start tracking or thinking about mixing. Give each step its due and the pieces will fit.

Second, play for the joy of it. If you get bogged down in worry or striving, you lose the main reason why you started playing in the first place. Hang on to the joy of your music: If you do, others will be able to hear it in the finished work.

And finally, don't worry about perfection. There's no such thing. Take your favorite Beatles song (or choose another artist if you don't dig the Beatles). That song could have been arranged, tracked, and mixed a hundred different ways and it would probably be every bit as good. They could have taken out the cool mistakes you've come to love and left in different mistakes, and it would still be the Beatles. Because the recording is frozen in time and you've become so accustomed to it, it's easy to think that it's perfect, but believe me, it isn't. Each song is a process, each process a chance to learn. Soon you'll be creating your own map of the landscape, and showing others the way.

crafting a soundscape

How to perfect your mixes

BY MITCH GALLAGHER

You've slaved and labored for days, weeks, even months to compose and craft your music, then you've spent even more time laying all that music down on your multitrack recorder or sequencer. You've come to the moment of truth—it is make or break time—*mixdown*.

It should be easy: Push the faders up, tweak a knob or two, and your tracks will swell forth from the studio monitors in glorious majesty, enveloping listeners in a panorama of sonic splendor … or not. Most often, not. What usually happens is that the tracks emerge from the monitors sounding okay, but they're sort of an amorphous mass. Various parts seem to be fighting each other, the low end is a bit muddy, and there's little spread and depth to the sound. There's not much clarity, and the subtle details are getting lost in the clutter. Let's take a look at what you can do to correct these problems as you mix your masterpiece.

EQ

One of the problems in many mixes is that tracks fight each other because they exist in similar frequency ranges. One reason for this is that the musical arrangement didn't account for the overlap in range. In other cases, the problem simply can't be avoided—occasionally the rhythm guitar is just going to have to overlap the lead vocal. Regardless of the reason for the conflict, equalization can be a lifesaver. Try EQing the combative parts with complementary boost and cut curves. For example, if your synth pad is covering up the lead vocal, cut the 500–2,000Hz range on the synth a bit, and slightly boost the vocal in the same range. This will provide the vocal with a little extra room to sit on top of the synth pad. Note that we're not talking about cutting and boosting by radical amounts here; a decibel or two in each direction should be all that's required.

Using EQ, I try to set each instrument up with its own range of frequencies where it can be most prominent in the mix. An example might be where the kick drum lives on the very bottom, bass guitar stacks on top of that, piano gets the lower mids with vocals sitting on top of it, then cymbals and strings ride on top.

Panning

In addition to giving each track its own place in the mix frequency-wise, give some attention to where each is placed in the stereo field. Certain instruments have locations where they're normally placed: Kick drum, bass guitar, and lead vocals typically are panned to the center, for example. Rules are meant to be broken, and you can certainly experiment with putting these kinds of things elsewhere in the stereo field. But it's likely that you'll want them to end up in the center. However, nothing says they have to be *exactly* in the middle. I often offset the panning of the kick drum and bass guitar by just a little bit in opposite directions from center. As far as the listener is concerned those sounds still come from the middle, but that tiny bit of positional offset seems to give the two tracks just a little bit more room to breathe without colliding.

If you have tracks that live in similar frequency ranges—say, electric guitar and B-3 organ—try panning them to different locations in the stereo field. I try never to have instruments that play in the same range in the same area of the stereo field, unless they're specifically doubling each other for a layered effect. The more you can put each track in its own location, the clearer your mix will be.

Be wary of having too many stereo or stereo-ized items in your mix; you'll end up with mush on the outside of the stereo field. Yes, the guitar player will want his lush stereo guitar tracks panned wide, but when you combine that with wide-panned stereo synth pads, strings, organ, and piano, there's just not room for it all. Consider narrowing the panning on some stereo items, or interlock the panning of two stereo tracks with one side of each signal panned wide, the other panned toward the center on the opposite side. It may be that all those signals don't necessarily *have* to be stereo. A mono part panned toward one side might be just as effective, and in fact, can sometimes seem more "present" in the mix because it doesn't take up as much room.

Effects

If you're having trouble getting tracks to sit well in a mix, consider adding some depth. Careful use of ambience effects such as reverb and delay can help move tracks forward and backward in the mix, improving mix depth and giving the tracks some room to breathe.

Reverb can be particularly effective for moving a track back in the soundstage, but be careful of overdoing it. We're not after a wash of effect here; rather, what we want is some ambience—as if you're hearing the sound from across the room instead of right in your face. I like to use a room preset with a short reverb time. Listen to the track dry, then gradually add a bit of 'verb until the track sounds as if it's backed away from you by a notch or two.

Delay, or echo, can have a similar effect, slightly reducing the presence of a sound in the mix and moving it back a pace or two. Try using a short delay, mixed down low behind the original sound. The point here isn't necessarily to hear a distinct echo effect; what we're after is a bit of reflection such as you might get when hearing a sound some distance from you in a large room.

If you can hear the effect distinctly in the mix when using this type of ambience, you've probably got too much of it dialed up. It's just right if you miss the ambience when you take it out, but it doesn't stand out as a separate item.

Mono

If your mix will be played over the radio, TV, or on low-end boom boxes with only one speaker, mono compatibility is certainly an issue. In reality, for most of us, our mixes will rarely be heard in mono. It's still worth checking your mix in mono, though. The main reason to do this is to ensure that you haven't created any strange phase anomalies during mixdown. (If things sound thinner or their tone changes—as opposed to just panned to the center—in mono than in stereo, you've got a phase problem.) But another reason is that if your sounds sit well in a mono mix, you can bet they'll be even clearer and better seated when you switch back to stereo. I commonly perform part of my EQing in mono for exactly this reason.

Pre-Planning

A lot of mixdown issues can be easily handled with a little pre-planning. For example, I recently recorded an instrumental piece that featured fretless bass and low-pitched hand drums. Since I knew the instrumentation in advance, when I tracked the bass, I focused on capturing a more midrangy tone than I might otherwise have gone for. As I recorded the hand drums, I kept the focus on their low frequencies. If you listen to either part solo, quite honestly they don't sound all that great. But when you combine the two parts together, the bass sits right on top of the drums, creating a full low-end blend that's perfect for the tune.

I could have waited until mixdown to EQ the bass and the drums to make them fit together. But I find there's always plenty to worry about during mixdown—

removing even one aspect from the process means there's that much less on my mind, and that much more attention that I can devote to the mix as a whole. Yes, yes, we've all heard that we should record "dry" and do EQing and processing during mixdown, but in the real world sounds are often tailored to some extent during the tracking stage.

Another aspect of pre-planning comes into play before you ever lay your finger on a piece of gear: musical arranging. All the EQ and processing in the world won't help to clear up a musical arrangement that's, shall we say, less than coherent. If you find that you just can't seem to get the mix the way you want it, step back and take a look at what's happening musically. Maybe a part can be dropped out, transposed, or rewritten to solve the problem.

Finally, nothing beats learning from the masters. Listen to a few well-mixed CDs, particularly those with dense arrangements, to see how the mix engineer put things together. How did the engineer EQ and place the sounds to avoid collisions and to let the important parts punch through? Did he use subtle ambience effects to place instruments in the mix?

Crafting the soundscape—getting everything to sit well in the mix—is a crucial stage in creating a stellar recording. With a little pre-planning, and careful use of equalization, stereo placement, and ambience effects, each of your tracks will have its own space to live in and will be able to peacefully coexist with its neighbors. Isn't that what life's all about?

flying solo

Working alone has both benefits and drawbacks

BY MITCH GALLAGHER

The ability for musicians to create a musical production entirely by themselves is one of the biggest blessings of the modern era, and at the same time one of the biggest curses. Working solo presents a unique set of problems and issues, which are highlighted when the medium is audio recordings. We're forced to function as both engineer and producer—and by the way, somewhere in there we're supposed to deliver a passionate musical performance. No problem, just divide the old brain into three independent parts and have at it . . . .

It seems simple: Set up the gear, push record, and lay it down. Unfortunately, the reality is more complex. Let's take a look at some ways to get better results when recording your own performances.

Set the Stage

We all know it's important to make the environment and experience comfortable for the artist. Just because the artist is *you* doesn't mean this is any less important, but many people working alone seem to forget this. As when you're working with other artists, take a look at the best way to position gear, give yourself enough room to comfortably move around, set yourself up with a favorite beverage, dim the lights, burn incense, whatever it takes to get you in the mood. The ultimate goal is to capture a great performance. All the techy stuff in the world won't matter if the performance is lame.

Control Noise

Most solo recordists end up doing all their work in the control room, right next to the ambient noise of their computer, hard drives, tape decks, amplifiers, and other gear with built-in fans or noisy moving parts. Take a look at your rig. Where are the sources of acoustic noise? Can they be moved into another room? Into a closet? At the very least away from the area where there will be open mics? Companies like Gefen Systems (www.gefen.com) make computer cable extenders that allow the CPU and hard drives to be located far away from the monitor and keyboard. Remote controls allow tape decks to be moved away from recording areas. I keep my digital multitrack recorders in a portable rack: As I'm setting levels, I've got them right there beside me where I can see the meters, but when I'm ready to record I pick them up and move them into the next room. If I'm really being down and dirty, I'll just throw heavy blankets over the rack to deaden the noise. (This is not recommended treatment for sensitive audio gear. Be *really* careful of overheating, and take the blankets off when you're not actually tracking!) Is there gear that you're not using for a particular take or recording? Turn it off until it's needed. If you're using directional mics, make sure you're positioning them to take maximum advantage of their noise rejection abilities. This may require slightly re-positioning yourself and your gear for best results.

Dynamics Control

Set your record levels very carefully, allowing for the fact that most people play a bit louder once the record light is glaring at them. Also leave yourself a bit of headroom for any unforeseen level peaks and louder-than-usual musical dynamics.

If you've got a limiter, patch it in the chain, and set it up to prevent overloading (digital gear is especially unforgiving of overly hot signals). Set it so that the threshold is a dB or so below the loudest peak your recorder can handle—I do this by trial and error in conjunction with the unit's meters—with a fast attack and release. You only want the limiter activated at the instant before distortion would otherwise occur, and to work only for as long as the peak lasts.

It may also help to patch in a compressor that's set up to pull back any strong peaks before they can cause distortion. Set it with a fairly high threshold, fast attack, and a 2:1–3:1 ratio. The idea isn't to compress your signal; rather it's to slightly reduce the level of any unusually high peaks. If you're free from worry about overloading the deck, you can quit watching the level meters out of the corner of your eye, and you'll be able to give a better performance.

Use Remote Controls

In addition to allowing you to move noisy recorders away from your recording area, remotes provide easy access to the buttons you'll need when recording; they're often easier to position near you than a bulky recorder or computer. Some recorders can accept footswitches for control of certain functions. For some reason I don't find they work well for me, but they may for you. Experiment.

Use Locate Points and Autopunch

If your recording system has locate points and autopunch features, put them to work—even if you're not punching in on a track. I'll often set up the autopunch on my recorders to drop me into record at the beginning of a track, and out at the end. I'll allow myself plenty of pre-roll to get ready, and let the punch function take care of the rest. Take the time before your session to program locate points so you can easily jump to the places you want without having to think about time and tape counters. It's all about removing as much "load" from your brain as possible so you can concentrate on the music.

Let It Roll

One of the beautiful things about tape-based MDMs (modular digital multitracks) is that the recording media is cheap. Get everything set up, start the tape rolling, and play take after take until you get one you like, or until the tape runs out. I find this works very well for me. On the first couple of takes, I'm still conscious of the machines, levels, and the mechanics of recording. By the third or fourth take, though, I can usually divorce myself from the machines and concentrate on my instrument or vocal. If you're playing to backing or previously recorded tracks, make yourself a tape with numerous back-to-back copies of the song, then hit record, and play along until you get a good take. If, at the end of the tape, you still don't have a complete take you're happy with, you'll have plenty of material to choose from for comping or editing together a master track. This tip will also work with a hard disk-based system (comping will certainly be easier), but you'll need a fair amount of free drive space. Keep in mind that if necessary you can always erase all those un-needed or botched takes and reclaim the space.

Be Objective

One of the hardest things to deal with when working alone is being objective about your performance. Very few of us can listen to music we've recorded and not have some kind of biased reaction to it. It's especially hard to listen back immediately after recording; every insignificant glitch, noise, and squeak jumps out in stark detail, overshadowing anything that might have been good about the take. In my experience, the best solution to this problem is time. I'll often record a tape full of performances of a song, then put it away for a week or two before listening back. When

I return to it with fresh ears and a slightly dulled memory of the minutiae, I find it far easier to focus on the music and overall picture without getting caught up in things no one else will ever hear or notice. No performance is ever perfect, and it's easy to miss the forest for the trees.

Reference Other Materials

As with performances, it's hard to be objective about audio production. We've all heard recordings where the person who engineers or produces has their own part turned up much louder in the mix than everything else or their vocal tracks are buried in the mix. In a band situation, you've got other ears to help combat this (of course, *everyone* in the band wants their part the loudest, but that's another issue). When you're working on your own, yours are the only ears around. One solution is to constantly reference other material as you're mixing. Find recordings you admire in a style similar to yours, and use them as a baseline for creating your own mixes.

Don't Work in a Vacuum

If you're the only person involved in creating a project, things can start to get unbalanced. Take the time to involve other people, even if only as listeners. This is a great way to get new ideas and a fresh perspective. I find that just listening to a song with other people colors the way I hear it compared to when I'm listening by myself. It may even help to have a friend or fellow recordist serve as a "co-producer." They don't necessarily have to be at the sessions, or even involved in the creation of the music, but using them as a sounding board can go a long way towards beating your own biases and focused perspective.

Be open-minded about the opinions you solicit, but realize that's what they are: opinions. In the end it's your music, and you've got to do what feels right to you.

Is going to all this effort to record by yourself worth it? Often it is. When you're working alone, you can take chances, try new things, make mistakes—no one will ever hear, so you can go for it! The freedom to unself-consciously open yourself to inspiration is a wonderful thing.

CHAPTER **17**

remixing 101

What's the buzz all about?
Take a step-by-step tour of the remixing process

BY GREG RULE

remixing is a red-hot topic these days. No matter the musical style, singers and bands are lining up to have their tracks remixed. Why? Remixes can add value to an artist's release, and can help their music penetrate into new markets. If you've been to a dance club, or if you've purchased singles or EPs, then you've probably heard remixed versions of songs. Cher's *Believe* CD-single, for example, contains her original album version plus ten remixes—each with its own distinct flavor.

But what exactly is a remix? What does the remixing process entail, and how can a computer musician such as yourself get a piece of the action? That's what this chapter will explore. Along the way, we'll discuss some of the tools and techniques in use by many leading remixers.

What Is It?

The word "remix" can be misleading. If you're familiar with how music is recorded, you know that musicians usually record separate parts (bass, drums, vocal, and so on) to separate tracks on a multitrack recorder. *Mixing* is the process in which the tracks in the multitrack recording are blended into the two-track (stereo) master recording that you'll hear on the radio. During mixing, a recording engineer applies equalization (changing the tone color), adds effects such as reverb and echo, and adjusts the volume levels of the various tracks so that all of the instruments can be heard properly. You might guess from this that a "remixer" would take the original multitrack recording and change the equalization and effects. Wrong! In most cases *only* the vocal is used from the artist's version. Everything else in the remix is created from scratch. Sometimes a song that was originally recorded in a major key will be changed to minor, or vice-versa. And often, in the process, the vocal tracks will be sped up, slowed down, or rearranged. As a result, a slow R&B ballad can be transformed into a pulse-pounding house track.

Simply put, remixing is an extensive and highly creative process. So much so, a "Remixer of the Year" category was added to the Grammys in 1998.

What You'll Need

There are many tools that can be put to good use in remixing: synthesizers, drum machines, turntables, effects processors, and the list goes on. But there are two main categories of gear that are essential to the process: a sampler (or digital audio software) and a sequencer.

Since remixing involves building new tracks around a pre-recorded vocal, you'll need a device to manipulate the vocal with. Standalone samplers (built by Akai, E-mu, Ensoniq, or Roland, for example) can be used alongside a sequencer, or you can accomplish both tasks under one roof by using a computer sequencer that has digital audio recording capabilities (Cakewalk Home Studio, Emagic Logic Audio MOTU Digital performer, Steinberg Cubase VST, and so on). Most software will work with the computer's own processor and built-in audio jacks (on the Macintosh) or a standard soundcard (on a PC), no additional hardware required. For better quality, you might want to consider adding a better soundcard or audio interface to your computer (see "Putting Your Studio Together" on page 37 for more on this). Whatever software or sampler you choose, make sure it can perform an editing function called time-compression/expansion, which we'll talk about later.

There's a third option that may be even more appealing to musicians who like to travel light: the groove box (see page 50). Roland's SP-808, for example, is a sampler and sequencer rolled into one, plus it has built-in effects and more. Yamaha's SU700 is another stand-alone groove box worth checking out, as are Akai's MPC2000, Ensoniq's ASR-X Pro, and Zoom's SampleTrak. I've seen world-class remixes done on all types of rigs—software and hardware.

How It's Done

The remix process almost always begins with the sampling or transferring of a raw vocal into a software program or sampler. If you're just starting out, and don't have access to quality vocal tracks, here's a suggestion: Look for *a cappella* (solo) vocal tracks on the B-sides of dance music 12-inch records, or on CDs. Alanis Morissette's multi-platinum *Jagged Little Pill*, for example, contains a hidden solo vocal track at the end of the disc. Just let the CD play for a minute or so past the last song, and you'll hear what I'm talking about. Use something like this as source material for your practice remixes. Another option is to purchase a remix-ready software program, such as Mixman Studio Pro (PC and Mac; www.mixman.com) and its accompanying D-Plates sample CDs. D-Plates provide isolated tracks from celebrity artists, such as Missy Elliott and Luscious Jackson.

Once the vocal is in the computer or sampler, it's time to think about the tempo of the remix. The one thing you don't want to do is make a remix that sounds too much like the original version. What's the point? When I remix, I like to take a song as far from the original as possible. That's why ballads are great candidates for uptempo dance remixes. But how do you change the tempo of the vocal without also changing its pitch? Earlier I mentioned a function called time-compression/expansion. This is the tool that allows you to do just that.

Using the above example, let's say your ballad vocal was originally recorded at 88 beats per minute (bpm). To get it up to house music pace, say, 125 bpm, you can use the time-compression feature of your sampler or software to increase the tempo of the vocal without adversely affecting its pitch. Most time-compression menus offer a "source" and "destination" tempo field. Just type in the before and after tempo, and sit back while the algorithm does its work. You can also use the tool in reverse to slow down the tempo. In our ballad example, we could go from 88 bpm down to 62.5. In this case, we'd layer the half-time vocal (62.5) over a double-time track (125). This doesn't always work, though, as the energy of the vocal can sound out of context against the fast track. Experimentation is the key.

Once the vocal is time-compressed or -expanded, the next step is to start building the remix around it. I like to begin with two tracks in my digital audio sequencer: one for the vocal and one for a reference drum loop. Often I'll record a beat with a drum machine, or sample a drum loop from a CD-ROM such as Big Fish's *Breakbeat* or East West's *XX-Large Killer* (see "Making Loop-Based Music" on page 137 for more). After the loop is sampled, I'll time-compress or -expand it if necessary, truncate it so there's no unwanted space at the beginning and end of the audio file, and then copy and paste it back-to-back for the length of the mix (see Figure 1). This will serve as my reference track, and form the foundation of the remix.

The next step is to start nudging the vocal phrases around so the timing is in perfect sync with the reference drum track. Almost always, this requires you to snip apart the vocal in many places, and then nudge each chunk individually. In some cases, I've even had to cut a line into individual words, and move each until the timing is right. This is probably the most tedious part of the remix process, but it's essential to spend the necessary time so the vocal is locked down and grooving.

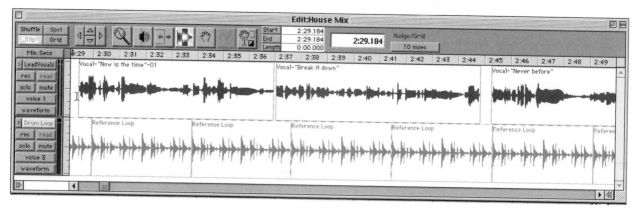

Figure 1 The beginning of a remix. In this Digidesign Pro Tools screenshot, you can see two tracks: One is a reference drum loop that's been copied a number of times so that it plays over and over; the other is the vocal track, which has been sliced into small pieces. Each piece is nudged until its timing lines up with the reference drum track.

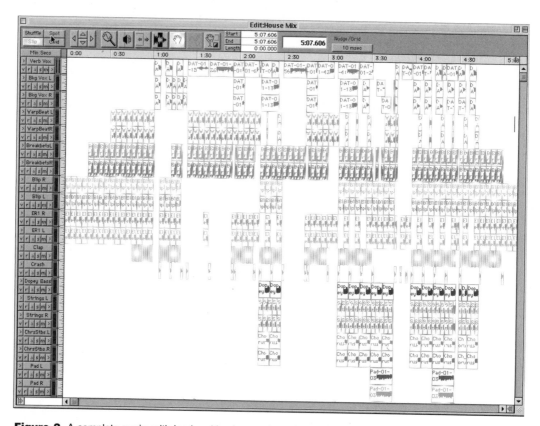

Figure 2 A complete remix, with lead and background vocals, drum loops, synth bass, chords, special effects sounds, and more. Can you identify the sections (intro, verse, chorus, bridge, etc)? Note the peak energy and density at the chorus locations.

With the vocal track now in sync with the beat, it's time to write and record the additional tracks: bass lines, synth chords, leads, special effects, drum patterns, fills, and so on. Generally I'll construct each section of the remix one at a time (intro, verse, chorus, bridge). In some cases I'll sequence the parts using the software's MIDI tracks, while other times I'll record the performances as audio tracks. Anything goes as long as the creativity flows.

Once the main tracks are sequenced and/or recorded (see Figure 2), I'll spend a session or two focusing on the arrangement. Should the chorus repeat twice after the second verse? Where should the breakdown occur, and for how many measures? How best can I segue from section to section? Lots of cut, copy, and paste occurs during this phase of the remix. Most of the remixes I do are intended to be played in clubs, so I make sure to put at least a minute of solo drums/percussion at the beginning and end of the mix, so DJs can easily mix into and out of the song.

Now that the arrangement is hammered down, it's time to mix our remix. Some remixers mix as they go, so to speak, which means that there really isn't much to do at this point. The volume levels have been adjusted, the effects have been applied, and so on. For me, I tend to wait until mixtime before getting serious about dialing in the effects and levels. Again, this is a subjective process. Do whatever works for you.

making loop-based music

*Making music with audio loops is more popular than ever
Here's how to get in on the fun!*

BY DOUG BECK

With the resurgence of dance music and the current success of artists such as Fatboy Slim, the Chemical Brothers, and the Basement Jacks, not to mention virtually every successful hip-hop record ever recorded, it's becoming obvious that loop-based composition is not just a fad that will quietly go away. The purpose of this chapter is to give you an introduction to how audio loops are used by some of today's most cutting-edge producers, composers and artists.

What's a Loop?

Let's start at the beginning. For the uninitiated, a loop is a short piece of audio that can repeat seamlessly. It can consist of a simple drum beat, percussion part, bass line, or guitar or synth part, or it can be an entire musical phrase, complete with vocals. Most loops are typically one to eight bars in length. The composer/producer (you) can use various audio loops in different combinations to create a new piece of music. Though loops can be obtained in many ways, sampling CDs are emerging as the preeminent source. Most sample CDs are royalty-free and license-free, which means you can use the included loops for any musical purpose, commercial or otherwise, without obtaining special permission or paying fees.

If you're just getting started with loop-based production, you may find that sampling CD-ROMs that contain pre-edited files are the easiest to work with. This is because the loop points in the audio have already been defined for you, which can be a great help. WAV and AIFF are the most common types of loop file formats. Just pop the CD into your computer's CD-ROM drive, load the file into your audio software, and you're ready to go. You can also download loop files from the Web (www.samplenet.com is one good source).

Sample CDs provide stereo audio; you can play them on your stereo just like any other CD of recorded music. But there is a catch: You'll have to capture and loop the audio yourself before you can work with it, and the art of looping certain types of audio can present a bit of a challenge for both beginners and experienced pros.

Why Loop?

It may be tempting to dismiss loop-based production as an easy out; you don't have to do the work of rehearsing, performing, recording live instruments, arranging, and mixing—at least not in the conventional sense. But as someone who has produced records using the more traditional approach, I can tell you that this argument actually embodies all the best reasons for using loops:

Performance. Let's face it. Most of us aren't virtuosos at every instrument. The idea of having great-sounding, wonderfully performed musical snippets to incorporate into a production is very tempting. Do you have the recording budget to bring in the best session musicians to cut some tracks for you? No? Loops put a virtual army of world-class pros at your disposal.

Variety. Sample CDs are available for pretty much every musical style. Some companies specialize in a particular area, while others offer broad selection from many genres. There are discs full of nothing but synth riffs, reggae beats, or percussion transitions, which offer a bewildering array of great choices for any production application. And if the dozens of new loop-packed CDs available every month are any indication, there will be no shortage of loops any time soon.

Sound quality. One of the greatest advantages of working with loops is that someone has already done the difficult and expensive engineering and recording for you. They've probably used those expensive microphones, EQs, tube compressors, and effects most of us can only dream about owning. Even better, the audio has been professionally mixed and mastered. While I have been disappointed in some instances, it's safe to say that the majority of sample CDs sound absolutely great.

Simplicity. If it sounds like loop-based production can yield great results, it can. And the best part is that there are some great tools available to make the process really fun and painless.

Getting Started

Okay, so you have a computer, you've just purchased a sample CD, and you're itching to get started. There are a few more basic items you'll want to consider before you jump in.

Soundcard. If you plan to import WAV or AIFF files directly from a CD-ROM into your computer, the potential degradation resulting from recording the audio input of an inexpensive soundcard is zero. However, if you want to capture audio from outside sound sources, or mix to an external tape deck, you may want to consider upgrading your computer's soundcard to something a bit better. Check out "Putting Your Studio Together" on page 37 for more on choosing a soundcard.

Software. Most popular sequencing software packages will allow you to import audio files, and many have some kind of time-compression and -expansion facility built right in. Time-expanding slows down the tempo of a loop, while time-compressing speeds the tempo up, without altering the pitch. The ability to compress or expand a loop is critical; you'll need to make the loops you select uniform with respect to tempo and key. This same technology can be used to change the pitch of a loop without altering its tempo. What all this means is that any loop can be put into any key at any tempo—at least in theory. The reality is that you can compress, expand, or pitch-shift a loop only so far before it starts to sound unnatural or just plain terrible. An alternative software technology designed specifically for altering the tempo of a loop is Propellerhead Software's *ReCycle*. Essentially, *ReCycle* chops up an audio file into many smaller files, based on peak hits. These tiny bits of audio are then squeezed together or stretched apart, which alters the tempo to whatever degree is desired.

Once the tempos of all the loops are the same, they can then be imported into your sequencer program. This is a simple step in most software environments, and usually just means choosing a track, clicking on "import," and selecting the loop. Once the loops are imported, you can cut and paste them just like measures of MIDI data. Interesting results can be achieved by layering various loops in different combinations, and by shifting the start point of a single loop forward or back. Of course, MIDI tracks and external devices such as multitrack tape decks can also be easily incorporated, making loops a flexible option to be used alone or in combination with other approaches to production.

If you're after a more dedicated loop-music production tool never fear: There have recently been some unbelievable breakthroughs in software technology for loop-based production. Programs such as Sonic Foundry's Acid (PC) and Mixman's Studio Pro (PC and Mac) stand out from the crowd by virtue of their simplicity. They make working with loops an incredibly fun and creative experience, even for a complete novice. In a nutshell, these programs are audio loop sequencers. Both programs allow you to audition, arrange, and layer different audio loops together to build tracks and songs, without any concern for pitch or tempo. How they manage to do this is a mystery to me, but the important thing is that it works and it's an absolute

Figure 1 Sonic Foundry's
Acid (Windows) is optimized for
working with loops. Here we
see a number of tracks, some
with repeating loops, some with
"single-shot" accents such as
crash cymbals. Acid takes much
of the drudgery out of creating
loop-based music, allowing you
to easily change both the tempo
and the pitch of a loop.

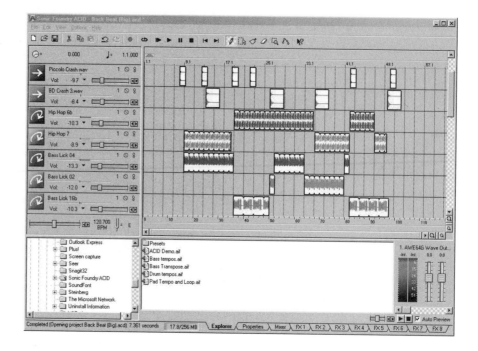

Figure 1 Sonic Foundry's Acid (Windows) is optimized for working with loops. Here we see a number of tracks, some with repeating loops, some with "single-shot" accents such as crash cymbals. Acid takes much of the drudgery out of creating loop-based music, allowing you to easily change both the tempo and the pitch of a loop.

blast to use. Each comes bundled with lots of music loops (drums and percussion, basses, guitars, keyboards, synths, etc.). There are also additional loop libraries available in many styles of music, and you can record your own audio directly into either program through your soundcard.

Advanced Audio Loop Editing

So now you want to take things a step further, and get into creating and editing your own loops. Maybe you want to take a loop from that sample CD you purchased and add effects, or chop it up and make it your own, so no one will be able to identify the original. Adding effects or editing an audio loop requires an audio editing program. There are many audio editing programs available for both the Mac and PC platforms, and though it would be impossible to talk about them all here, we can provide some ideas to get you started.

Basically, all of these programs function in a similar fashion: You import any WAV or AIFF file into the audio editor from your hard drive or from a sample CD. (Or, you can record from an audio CD or other source directly into the audio editor through your computer's soundcard.) You can then see the loop graphically and perform various functions on it, such as reversing it, shortening it, or cutting it up and reassembling its pieces in a different order. Depending on the software program, you can add effects to the loop, such as filtering or reverb. When shopping for an audio-editing program, it's a good idea to find out what types of effects are included with the package. On the PC platform I recommend Sonic Foundry's Sound Forge

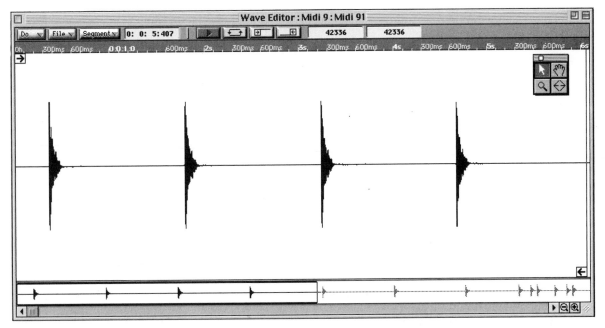

Figure 2 Once you have a loop in your computer, you may need to clean it up a bit. In this case, we'll want to use audio editing software to delete the dead air to the left of the first cowbell hit. That way, when the loop is repeated, it will play with the correct rhythm.

XP and Syntrillium Software's Cool Edit. On the Mac, check out Macromedia's Sound Edit 16, BIAS's Peak, and TC Works' Spark. All of these programs will allow you to edit and add effects to your audio loops.

Get Looped

Powerful technology for loop-based production becomes less expensive and more user-friendly every year. Whether you're looking to make music exclusively with loops or just want to incorporate a loop or two into your latest production, it's never been easier or more accessible for producers and amateurs at any level. In fact, one of the greatest features of loop-based music is that it's so easy to do. Still, however impressive the technology, and however rich the source of available loops may be, the music that results is still strictly a matter of your own ideas—the possibilities are truly endless. The future of music looks bright ... and more than a little bit "loopy."

ten ways to enjoy your studio

Looking to have fun, learn something, or maybe even make a buck or two in your home studio? Try these suggestions!

BY JIM BORDNER

ome studio owners are usually driven by two primary desires: to get better at making music, and to acquire cooler tools to do it with.

But we spend so much time working alone, recording our own songs and dealing with our own stylistic biases, it can be difficult to make progress. And for most of us, diverting buckazoids from the New Furnace Fund to grab that wicked rackmount goodie is just not an option.

So let me suggest ten things to do with your studio that you might not have considered. Each one offers opportunities to expand musically by taking on new styles or working with other musicians. And most have the potential to make you a few shekels, too—which you can then spend without guilt on groovy toys.

1. Produce demos for singers and songwriters. This is rewarding work. You get to meet people with similar goals, coach and encourage them, and make friends with some amazingly talented artists. The work can be as simple as directing a singer performing to a karaoke tape, or as involved as creating entire arrangements for original songs.

You can meet your potential clients in all the places you'd expect: clubs, music stores, karaoke bars, churches. Put the word out among some friends that you're looking for opportunities. Strike up a conversation with that impressive singer at open mic night. Work with people you admire and who possess a personality that matches up with your own. Even if you end up charging for your services, remember this is supposed to be fun.

If you decide to make some money, charge an hourly rate for karaoke-type work, plus the cost of the copies you make of the finished song. If you're arranging and producing original songs, work out a per-project price with your client.

2. Make a holiday album. This was my first "real" project in my first home studio. My relatives loved it, and most of them had no idea what I was capable of ("Oh, I think Jimmy still plays the piano or something, doesn't he?"). Seeing them slightly amazed at my developing skill was a nice little Christmas bonus.

Choose traditional songs that hold some interest for you, musically or otherwise. Approach them in a non-traditional way, giving them some of your own personality. One of the benefits of this project is the invigorating stretch it will give your musical muscles.

It doesn't have to be radio-ready. My holiday album was distributed on cassettes with hand-written J-cards to 14 people. Start early so you're not rushing to finish after Thanksgiving. Maybe the record will turn out so well that you'll want to try selling CD copies at local stores!

3. Program background music. If you have a CD player and cassette deck or CD recorder in your studio, you're ready for this one. Make a deal with stores or restaurants to act as a "music consultant." Work with them to create a playlist of music that fits their establishment and compile a list of CDs. They buy the CDs, and you sequence custom-programmed music for their business.

Don't succumb to the temptation to scrounge your source material from the library or from your own CD collection. It's not kosher, copyright-wise, because you're re-selling someone else's work. And encourage your clients to pay the appropriate BMI and ASCAP license fees (they probably already do).

Anytime you're in a restaurant that's playing a radio in the background, approach the owner or manager and ask them how may times they've heard ads for their competitors played on the radio in their own store. That usually gets their attention. You should charge a straight hourly fee for editing, and a consulting fee if you can get it. Restaurants are often interested in trading services (a great way to grab some free meals at your favorite place).

4. Make music for someone to perform to. Gymnasts, fitness competitors, skaters, and many other athletes perform to music, either original music or edited from existing recordings. Skaters and gymnasts tend to choose an existing tune and have it edited to fit their performance. You're all set if you have a computer editing system.

Fitness competitions are fueled by high-energy tracks, where pieces from records are mixed with original elements, like a remix. If you're into this kind of production, you can start networking through gyms and fitness centers: You'll find the people who want these tracks leading aerobics classes.

Riding competition, or "dressage" as it's called, is performed to edited or original music with a twist. The music changes tempo several times, and must be precisely matched to an individual's horse's natural tempo when walking or cantering or whatever. It's a great opportunity to produce original music, or a fun editing job if your studio can do time compression and expansion of audio tracks. Promote yourself through the boarding stables.

If you decide to charge for a project like this, know that clients will be unique in their needs and budget. Work out a per-project price.

5. Write and record a song for a loved one. If you want to give someone a truly special gift, you will *never* please them more than by writing and recording a song for them. It's the thought that counts, and what could be more thoughtful?

It's a great way to mark milestones: an important birthday, a wedding or anniversary, whatever. Make notes on everything you know about the subject, and then take some time to talk to other friends or relatives. Make it more of a musical challenge for yourself by matching the giftee's taste in music: If they love country, make it a country song; if they have a lot of Sinatra in their collection, go for that smoky nightclub feel.

If there's a party planned to mark the milestone, you could play the song live before giving them the tape with your recorded version. Believe me, they'll never forget it.

6. Help out a school music program. Every school has bands and choirs, and they all need to be recorded. All you need are some microphones, a small mixer, a stereo recorder you can haul around (DAT is generally best), and a basic knowledge of stereo miking techniques.

If you do this for the sheer fun of it (or because you have a kid in the school band), you'll be rewarded only with undying gratitude and a standing invitation to come back next year and do some more.

If your skill and equipment are of a professional grade, you can charge an hourly rate for the recording. Or offer turnkey service by mastering the recordings and acting as the school's middleman with the CD factory, marking up the cost of duplication a few percent to cover your time. One guy I know makes a living at this by offering the recording service for free, handling the duplication, taking orders for the album from parents, paying a percentage of the purchase price back to the school for the arts fund, and keeping the rest. He has his own little record company, in effect, and a captive buying audience. If you handle the CD distribution, be aware that you need to license the mechanical rights to the music through the Harry Fox Agency in New York (www.nmpa.org/hfa.html, 212-370-5330).

7. Produce "on hold" tapes. Many businesses already have a service that provides them with recorded messages for audio-on-hold. But some still use a radio—or worse, one of those cheesy synths that auto-generate a sort of beeping kindergarten Bach.

Maybe you have a friend who runs a retail store or a professional office that could use this service. Let them know they're missing a good opportunity to communicate with their customers, and see if you can't convince them to give it a try. On-hold messaging is typically updated quarterly, but some retail stores like to update monthly to promote in-store specials. You might have to work pretty cheap for a while to get them to try it, but once you have some samples produced, you can go after bigger, wealthier fish. Maybe someday you'll even take on the established competition.

8. Make practice tapes for students. Do you know players who also teach? You can help them and their students by producing "music-minus-one" rhythm tracks that fit their lesson plans. The students then have a ready reference for soloing practice.

If you do this just for fun, you have no licensing issues. But if you sell the tapes and the tunes are not all originals, you need to get clearances. The Harry Fox Agency recommends that you contact publishers directly, as HFA's standard fee for mechanical rights would be prohibitively high. Many publishers may not require payment for this sort of use.

If you decide to turn pro, put several tunes on a tape and sell them to students for $20 or so, with a percentage going to the teacher. It doesn't sound like much, but if you have five teachers with 30 students each, it'll add up. You could even do it with a copy of PG Music's Band-in-a-Box and a General MIDI (GM) synth to turn orders around quickly.

9. Preserve a family reunion. This is more fun than the usual boring home video of a family event. Take a portable tape recorder to a party or reunion, either DAT or cassette, and "interview" the attendees. Then take the tape home and use your computer editor to cut the interviews down to a ten- to 15-minute montage. Compose some music to underscore the interviews, and send cassettes of the finished program to everyone who was there. You get more interesting results than you would with a video camera (people tend to simply wave and mug on video, but for the tape recorder they have to *talk*), and your friends and family will love hearing those familiar voices blended with your music.

10. Produce a cover or parody. Hey, it doesn't *all* have to be original. A great way to learn arranging and production is to rework an existing song. Choose one of your all-time favorites and see how close you can come to capturing its feel (three years and I'm still perfecting my cover of "Walk Away, Renee"). Or learn some new licks by taking something that you don't like all that much and writing a parody. Those Weird Al records demonstrate some pretty sophisticated production chops.

There you go: ten ways to enjoy your studio. If you decide to make a few extra bucks with any of these techniques, you can plow your profits back into gear until you and your room are ready to turn pro. Expand your capabilities along with your reputation, and finally quit your day job and make music all day.

But even if you decide just to play for fun and glory, I urge you to widen the scope of the things you try and things you record. The greatest joy a musician can have is successfully learning something new. And taking joy in our work is the whole reason why we do this in the first place, isn't it?

putting your music online

BY SCOTT R. GARRIGUS

or many of us, the process of creating and recording our music is its own reward. While few of us would turn down Warner Bros. or Sony Records if they came calling, becoming a rock star isn't really our goal. Still, wouldn't it be nice to get your music out to a larger audience than your immediate family and friends? Wouldn't it be cool if the masses could enjoy your tunes? And what would be wrong with maybe making a buck or two off of your efforts?

Until recently, exposing your music to a large audience was a costly proposition best left to the professionals. But as with many aspects of modern life, the Internet has changed the picture. Using the Web you can make your music available to an incredibly large potential audience. No one can guarantee that just posting your songs to the Web will result in people hearing them or in your making any money, but hey, at least there's a reasonable self-promotion avenue available for you to exploit!

Putting music on the Web may seem like an arcane task best left to cellardwelling Web hackers with questionable personal hygiene, but in fact it's a pretty easy task. Let's take a look at what it takes to prepare your music for the online experience.

To get things started, you're going to need your music in some finished form. It could be on cassette, DAT tape, or living as audio files on your computer's hard drive. If your music isn't ready for listeners, getting it recorded is the first task facing you. If your tunes are recorded and ready to go, then you're well underway. The next step is to figure out whether you want to create your own Web site or let someone do that work for you.

When in Doubt, Delegate

The easiest way to get your music online is to have someone else do it for you. Many Web sites offer online promotion and distribution for independent musicians (see "Popular Promo Sites"). You simply fill out an agreement, tell them about yourself, provide a photo or two of your smiling face, and supply them with your finished

Popular Promo Sites

While there are literally hundreds of music-related sites on the Internet—not including the thousands of sites devoted to individual musicians and groups—we would be remiss if we didn't mention a few of the more popular ones. Some of these sites offer a full line of services; all you need to do is supply them with your music, and they'll take care of giving you a Web presence. Others will host your music for free, but you'll need to take care of creating your own audio files, etc. Even if you decide to create your own Web site, it might still be a good idea to place your music on some of the sites listed here. It will help steer traffic to your site and expose your music to a wider audience.

www.amp3.com   www.iuma.com

www.besonic.com   www.mp3.com

www.cmj.com/mp3   www.resortrecords.com

www.dmusic.com   www.ubl.comx

www.goodnoise.com   www.y2k-music.co.uk

music. They'll convert your recordings into the right types of digital audio files and create a page on their site containing the information about you and your music. They'll offer your songs for download to visitors either for free or a fee, depending on the agreement. Some offer short demo clips to visitors to give them a taste of your music, and then sell copies of your CD (if you have one).

In exchange for these services, you'll have to fork over some cash. Some sites charge a set annual fee that can range from $99 to $300. Others won't charge you anything unless you actually sell some music; then they'll take a percentage of the sale—sometimes up to 50 percent. This type of arrangement can be worth it if you don't want to hassle with putting a Web site together yourself.

If you decide to go with one of these promo sites, you can exit this article here—no need to read any further. But if you're interested in doing some or all of the tasks involved in putting your music online yourself, read on.

In addition to the "commercial" promo sites discussed above, there are sites that let you promote your music for free. They give you a free Web page so that you can post information about your music as well as a link to your Web site (if you have one). And they'll give you free disk space so that you can offer your songs to visitors for download. But since the services are free, you'll usually have to take care of all the details yourself. This includes converting your recordings into digital audio files.

You can also choose to create your own Web site and post your songs to it. Creating a Web site is beyond the scope of this article. If you need information on how to create a Web site, check out *Creating Cool Web Pages with HTML* by Dave Taylor (http://intuitive.com/coolweb) and *Poor Richard's Web Site* by Peter Kent (www.poorrichard.com).

Let's take a closer look at what's required to get your music ready for the online experience. We'll also sift through the more popular Web audio formats, and take a quick glance at what's required to put the audio files on your site.

What Do I Need?

You probably already have much of the gear and software you need to get your songs ready to go online (assuming, as mentioned above, that your songs are recorded and ready to be distributed). For starters, you'll need a computer, soundcard, and digital audio editing software (see "Guide to Studio Equipment" on page 39 and "Software for the Studio" on page 65 for more on this).

To put your music online, you also have to have access to the Internet. This usually means forking over $20 a month for an ISP (Internet Service Provider) account. But these days a number of companies provide free Net access. In exchange, they put a small ad banner on your screen while you're online. A small price to pay for free access, in my opinion, so you may want to check it out. One of the better-known services is NetZero (www.netzero.com).

If you're going to create your own site, you'll need somewhere to store your Web pages and your digital audio files. The agreement you have with your ISP may entitle you to storage space on their Web server. If not, you can sign up with a dedicated Web hosting service, which can cost $20 or more each month. But as with ISPs, there are companies out there who provide free Web hosting in exchange for placing ads on your Web pages. Yahoo! GeoCities (http://geocities.yahoo.com) and Xoom.com (http://xoom.com) are two; there are others as well. Before signing up with a Web hosting service, check to make sure that they're set up to allow your fans to download audio files in the format(s) you'd like to supply, and that the amount of space you'll need for the audio files on the site won't cost you extra.

If your songs already exist as sound files on your computer, you can skip to "What Format?" below. Otherwise you'll need to get your music into your computer. The process of converting the songs from tape or CD to digital audio files is quite easy. Simply connect your tape or CD player to your computer's soundcard and play each song one at a time, recording them using your digital audio recording software. Then save them as 16-bit/44.1kHz resolution WAV or AIFF files. These are the standard digital audio file formats on the PC and the Mac, respectively.

What Format?

After you've finished converting your songs into digital audio files in WAV (in Windows) or AIFF (on the Mac) format, you need to decide what file format(s) you're going to use to put them online. Technically, you could upload your files as is, but not only will you quickly run out of space on your Web site, no one will download the files because they'll be much too big. CD-quality (16-bit/44.1kHz) stereo audio takes up about 10MB of disk space per minute. This means that a five-minute song will be around 50MB in size. It could take hours for someone to download a song of that size, even if they had a fairly speedy modem—although cable modems and DSL are becoming more common, you can't assume that visitors to your site will have broadband connect speeds. To get around this problem, audio files are usually data-compressed down to a more reasonable size using a variety of audio technologies and file formats. Each of these has its strengths and weaknesses, so you may want to offer your songs in more than one format.

MP3. If you'd like to make sure your files retain near-CD-quality sound while only taking up about 1MB (compared to 10MB) of disk space per minute, then consider using the MP3 format. MP3 uses what is known as "lossy" data compression. This means that it reduces file size by throwing away parts of the audio signal that listeners theoretically won't miss. In practice this works surprisingly well, although no one claims that MP3s are suitable for critical, golden-ear listening. What you end up with is a much smaller file that can be sent quickly over a modem connection. Your listeners will still have to spend some time downloading the files, but with MP3 it will take minutes instead of hours. The other advantage is that many computer users are familiar with MP3 files, and will likely have the necessary software for playing them back.

Streaming audio. If you want to provide your listeners with the added convenience of not having to wait for your audio files to download, then consider using a streaming audio format. Streaming audio allows your listeners to immediately hear your music while it's being downloaded. This means no more waiting for downloads, but it can mean lower sound quality. Users downloading your music will also have to have the necessary player software in order to listen to your songs. In most cases, this isn't a big problem: The players are free and readily downloadable on the Web.

A number of streaming audio technologies are in use, the most popular being RealAudio, Liquid Audio, QuickTime, and Windows Media Technologies. As with MP3 files, streaming technologies use lossy compression to reduce file sizes to a more modem-friendly level.

As of this writing, RealAudio is the most popular format being utilized, with over 60,000,000 downloads of the RealPlayer software. Many feel, however, that the best-sounding format is Windows Media Technologies. Using WMT you can potentially achieve FM stereo radio-like quality on a 28.8K modem connection, though many factors can affect the final quality of the audio the end user receives.

Be aware that there's a hidden aspect to streaming formats: The audio files must be stored on a server that has software capable of providing streaming capabilities. In most cases, you'll pay extra for streaming capabilities.

Pre-Processing

If you plan on using a data-compressed audio format, you may want to consider tweaking the sound of your files before you encode them (turn them into streaming files). Creating streaming files directly from your original WAV or AIFF files may work just fine. But since the streaming audio formats use such massive amounts of data compression, a little pre-processing usually helps.

File editing. The first thing to do is to use your audio editing software to remove any dead air from the beginning and end of your song. Once your file is edited, make a copy of it. This copy will be useful later as a reference point.

DC offset removal. Before you make any changes to the sound, you should remove any DC offset that might have crept in during the recording. DC offset is low-frequency, inaudible noise that usually occurs because of an improperly grounded soundcard or a bad connection between the soundcard and a tape player, etc. If you don't remove DC offset, your files may end up noisier when you encode them. Most audio editing software programs offer DC offset removal functions.

Compression. This isn't the same as data-compressing a file to make it smaller for downloading or streaming. Audio compression affects the volume of the sound, not the size of the file. This type of compression takes the loudest sections of a sound and reduces their level while at the same time raising the level of the quietest sections.

Compression reduces the dynamic range of the music, giving it a more even volume level, which is better when it comes time for encoding.

Your digital audio software should include some type of dynamics processing function that allows you to set a compression ratio (see Figure 1). Usually, a good ratio is between 2:1 and 4:1. The setting you use will vary with the content of the audio, but if you can get away with a 2:1 setting, that's usually best. Too much compression can make the music sound dull and lifeless. Use the reference copy of your audio file you created earlier to assess the effects of the compression. If the compressed version sounds worse than the reference copy, back up and try again.

EQ. Because the streaming audio encoding process removes a lot of the high-frequency (treble) portion of an audio signal, some EQ (equalization) is usually needed. Again, your digital audio software should include an EQ function. As when you added compression, break out your reference audio file to assess the effects of the EQ. Once you've encoded the file (see below) you'll want to listen to it to check the effects of your EQ. Experiment with different EQ settings until the encoded file sounds good to you. Often you'll find yourself giving the audio a midrange boost of about 6dB at around 2.5kHz (see Figure 2).

Normalize. The last step before encoding is to normalize the audio file. Normalization raises the volume of an audio signal as high as it can go without causing any distortion. If your software allows it, normalize your files to 95%, rather than 100%. This will leave a small amount of headroom in case the encoding process needs it.

Once you're finished processing, save the file (be sure to use a new name so you keep the original file intact) in WAV or AIFF format, and you're ready to encode.

Encoding

To encode your files, you'll need special software. Depending on the file format you've chosen, the software may be free, or it may not. In some cases the CODEC (the software that encodes the music) may be built into your audio editor, or it may be included with you audio editor. The actual encoding process varies with each format, but documentation that will step you through it comes with most of the software out there. Many times, the default encoder settings work just fine.

MP3. There's plenty of free software available for encoding MP3 files—your digital audio editing software may even be able to export files in MP3 format. One of the most popular free encoders for the Windows platform is MusicMatch Jukebox (www.musicmatch.com). Mac users are particularly fond of the Mpecker Encoder—yes, that's its real name (www.anime.net/~go/mpeckers.html). You may also want to

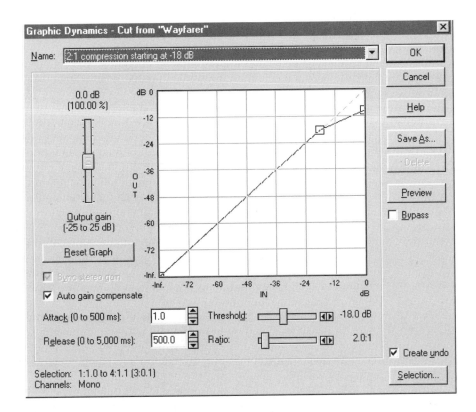

Figure 1 Audio compression affects the volume of the sound, not the size of the audio file. Compression takes the loudest sections of a sound and reduces their level by a certain amount. This gives you room to turn up the entire signal, raising the overall average level. In this example, signals above the −18dB threshold will be compressed with a 2:1 ratio.

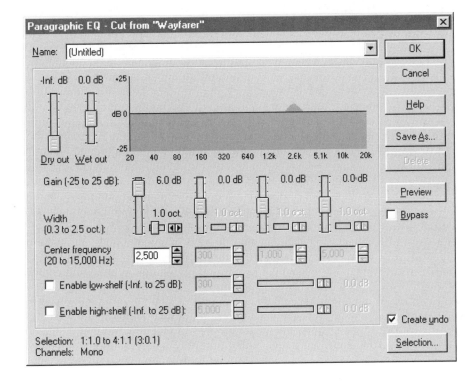

Figure 2 To compensate for the loss of brightness that can occur when a sound file is converted into streaming audio, equalize the file prior to encoding it. In this case, a 6dB boost is being added at 2.5kHz.

consider spending a little money on one of the commercial MP3 encoders. Why? Because encoders aren't all created equal. While there are some excellent freeware encoders available, their commercial competitors tend to produce better sounding files in a shorter amount of time. One is AudioCatalyst (www.xingtech.com), which is available for both the PC and the Mac.

RealAudio. To encode files in RealAudio format, you have to go directly to the company that created the technology, RealNetworks. They provide both free and commercial encoding software. In this case, the commercial encoder doesn't generally produce better-sounding files in a shorter amount of time. Rather, it provides a number of handy features not found in the free version. For a comparison of the two versions, check out www.real.com. The free encoder (RealProducer Basic) and the commercial encoder (RealProducer Plus) are available for both Windows and the Mac.

QuickTime. Although Apple's QuickTime is more often used for video content, the latest version of this technology sounds as good as it looks. QuickTime can produce high-quality streaming audio, but unfortunately there aren't any free encoders available. Still, at $29.95, the QuickTime Pro encoding software (available for both Windows and the Mac) isn't terribly expensive. You can purchase a copy online at www.apple.com.

Media Technologies. The only totally free streaming audio format on the market today is Media Technologies from Microsoft. A whole suite of free tools for creating Media Technologies files is available for download at www.microsoft.com. There's just one catch: The tools are available only for Windows. If you want to encode Media Technologies files on the Mac, you'll have to fork over $599 for Terran Interactive's Media Cleaner Pro software (www.terran-int.com). However, free players are available for both Mac and Windows platforms.

Liquid Audio. The great thing about Liquid Audio (www.liquidaudio.com) is that it's a secure format, which means people won't be able to make copies of your music files and distribute them without your permission: The tracks are "watermarked" to allow ownership tracking and encrypted so that only the authorized listener can play them. Only the player software is free. The encoding software for this format is Liquifier Pro (available for Mac and Windows); visit the Liquid Audio site for current pricing.

Post-Process

After you've recorded, processed, and encoded your files, it's time to get them up on the Web. Posting your files to your site is pretty easy. All you need to do is upload your files to your Web server, and then create standard links to them on your Web page(s). The HTML code for the link might look something like this:

```
<a href="mysong.mp3">Click to hear my song!</a>
```

As mentioned earlier, in order to use streaming audio formats, your Web host's server will need to have special streaming software installed; usually you'll be charged a premium to use this capability. Using the server software makes the files stream (or download) reliably, and allows a large number of listeners to access the files at once.

Thanks! I'll Try It

Putting your music online is a great way to make it available to a potentially huge listening audience. If your music is recorded and ready to be heard by the anxiously awaiting masses, why not join the thousands of musicians who have already put their music online? Who knows, you might even make a buck or two—would that be such a bad thing?

creating your own audio CDs

With a computer and a few pieces of software and hardware, it's easy to create audio CDs at home

BY ROB MCGAUGHEY AND MITCH GALLAGHER

U p until the very recent past, unless you were an artist signed to a major label, distributing your music to the public—or even to a few friends or family members—was a tricky thing. About the only medium available to you was the venerable analog cassette tape. You could use DAT tape, but few people outside pro studios had DAT machines. Vinyl LPs and singles were also an option but required duplication at a commercial duplication facility. So you were stuck with cassette tape, with its limited frequency response and noise levels. With cassette, you never knew quite *what* your music would sound like on the end-user's system.

With the dramatic reductions in the cost of computers, hard drives, CD burners, and blank CD media, those problems are a thing of the past. Delivering music on CD allows for clean, quiet audio reproduction, without the problem of limited frequency response, and without the variables of tape bias, noise reduction, and poor machine alignment. It's finally possible for home studio owners to deliver music on a medium that's as good as what the big-buck pros use. Let the rejoicing begin! (Of course, this also means you can no longer blame your delivery media for the sound of your project, but that's an entirely different topic . . . .)

For those who want to burn audio CDs at home, there's a wide array of options available for both PCs and Macs. Computer-based CD-burning systems are quite versatile and with the proper software can be used to create not only audio CDs but CD-ROMs, photo CDs, and video CDs. They're an excellent low-cost data-backup solution.

Four basic components are necessary for creating a CD from a personal computer: the computer, a hard drive for storing audio data, software to format the audio data, and blank CD media. Let's take a look at each of these items.

• Computer Requirements

PC: Any 100MHz or faster Pentium class machine is suitable for burning audio CDs. You should be running Windows 95 or later and will need at least 16MB RAM (32MB or more is highly recommended). Faster computers (>266MHz) with 32MB or more RAM are best, especially when burning a CD at higher speeds. For the best performance and reliability, consider adding a SCSI controller card to your computer so you can use a SCSI hard drive and CD burner. Good quality SCSI cards are available starting well under $100. Many newer PCs also offer support for USB CD burners.

Mac: Any Power Mac with 32MB RAM should be fine. If you're using an older Mac (a Quadra or other 68040-based machine), you can still burn CDs from image files (see glossary). OS 7.5 or later is recommended. With OS 8.5 or later you may want to increase the amount of RAM to 64MB or higher. Most Macs support SCSI CD burners, although iMacs and the recent G3s/G4s don't have built-in SCSI connectors. For those machines, USB and (in the case of the G3/G4) FireWire drives should work fine.

• Hard Drive

You'll need a hard drive that's capable of recording audio from whatever source you're planning to use and keeping up with the CD burner. Look for an access time of 10ms or faster. With nearly all modern drives, there shouldn't be any problem. Parallel port drives may work but aren't recommended when burning a CD.

Hard drives stop every so often and check themselves out; this is called thermal recalibration. If your hard drive chooses to recalibrate when you're recording audio tracks or burning CDs, then you could be in trouble. Most CD burners have a RAM buffer that will help prevent problems with the hard drive keeping up, but this isn't always enough. Most modern hard drives deal with thermal recalibration in such a way that it doesn't affect data transfers to a CD burner, but with older drives this can be an issue. Make sure your hard drive deals with thermal recalibration appropriately. Again, with newer drives this won't be an issue.

Plan to reserve plenty of hard drive space for your files when burning CDs. A standard audio CD requires 44.1kHz/16-bit stereo format files, which use approximately 10MB of hard drive space per minute. This means a standard 74-minute audio CD will require around 740MB of available space. If you're creating an image file to burn the CD from (see below), then double your hard disk requirements. In this case, the same 74-minute audio CD would require almost 1.5GB of disk space (740MB for the source audio files and 740MB for the image file).

CD Labeling Systems

CD Labeling Software

Manufacturer	Product	Price	Platform	Web site
Data Becker	CD Labelmaker	$19.95	Win	www.databecker.com
Neato	CD Labeler	$29.95	Mac/Win	www.neato.com
Stomp	CD Stomper	$39.95	Mac/Win	www.cdstomper.com

CD Printers

Manufacturer	Product	Price	Platform	Web site
Affex	Apprentice	$895	Mac/Win	www.affex.com
Affex	SK7 Plus	$1,695	Mac/Win	www.affex.com
Affex	CD Artist Plus	$2,495	Mac/Win	www.affex.com
Primera	Signature III	$1,495	Mac/Win	www.primeratechnology.com

Tired of searching through stacks of identical-looking golden CD-R discs looking for the one you want? Want your finished CDs to look more professional? If you have a printer and a computer then you can easily make nice labels and jewel box inserts. Several companies have packages that help you design CD artwork, print it, and apply the labels to your CDs. Most packages include templates that support common software programs such as Microsoft Word, Adobe Pagemaker, QuarkXpress, and Corel Draw, and generic templates that can be imported to just about any word processor or graphics program. Some CD-burning software packages, such as Roxio's Easy CD Creator (www.roxio.com), also allow you to design and print CD labels and jewel-box inserts. This lets you take care of the entire CD creation process in one program. Templates are also included for creating CD jewel case inserts, and even customizing the spines. Stick-on CD labels can be purchased in most computer supply stores. These can be inserted into any ink jet or laser printer. Some packages (such as those from Neato and Stomper) include a label applicator that helps you perfectly center labels on the disc and apply them without any wrinkles.

If you really want to get serious about CD labeling, there are ink jet printers that can print directly on the surface of the CD-R disc. These systems are somewhat expensive, but the finished product can look very professional. Note that most of these printers require special CD-R media with a white or silver coating on the print side. If you plan to burn and distribute a lot of CD-Rs, then one of these may be worth the investment.

For quick, down-and-dirty CD labeling, it's hard to beat a CD-R pen. These allow you to write directly on the CD, which is fine for many applications and saves the time of creating and printing labels. Be careful, though: It might seem like you could just use any felt-tip pen for writing on CDs, but this isn't the case. The ink in some pens can penetrate and destroy CD-R media, so it's important to get a pen that's safe. Apogee Electronics (www.apogeedigital.com) makes one.

Data Backup

The one thing we know for certain about computers and hard drives is that they will crash. Unfortunately, it's impossible to predict exactly when this will happen, so it's important to back up important data regularly. A CD burner makes a great, low-cost backup and archiving system for your computer data. Many of the same programs that make audio CDs are capable of doing data backups as well.

Either CD-R or CD-RW formats work well for backup and archiving. CD-RW works especially well for backup because you can reuse the discs, but the discs are more expensive and can be modified or erased, so they're less attactive for permanent archiving. Since CD-R discs are inexpensive, they make a great permanent backup/storage/archiving solution. A CD can hold up to 650MB of data.

• Software

You'll need software to format the audio files for the CD burner. Make sure that the software you choose supports the CD burner that you have or are considering buying. Virtually all manufacturers of CD-burning software publish a list of the drives they support; start with a visit to their Web site to find out if your drive is on the list. If you're concerned about compatibility, you may want to take advantage of bundles offered by some companies that include the CD burner, CD burning software, and other useful utilities.

Check out the chart on page 163 for pointers to some manufacturers of CD burning software. For basic use creating audio CDs for yourself and your friends, any of these packages should serve you well. If you want to get tweaky about song spacings, relative volume levels between songs, crossfades between tracks, and sub-index points, or if your goal is to burn a CD that you'll send off for mass replication, then check the feature lists carefully. You probably need to invest in one of the higher-end products.

Some of these packages can also assist you in creating CD labels and jewel box inserts, or have special features designed to allow you to convert MP3 files to audio CDs, remove noise and pops from LPs, and to create your own "greatest hits" CDs. Some will also allow you to burn CD-ROMs that you can use as backups of your computer data (see "Data Backup" above).

• CD Burner

There are two basic formats of CD burners on the market today that are capable of producing a standard audio CD. CD-R is a write-once format that cannot be erased or re-recorded. CD-RW is a rewritable format that, when used with special rewritable discs, can be erased and rewritten with new data. Most CD-RW burners offer the

The Need for Speed

CD burners are rated at "x" speeds, which relate to how fast they can burn a disc. When working with audio CDs, 1x refers to real time. A five-minute song, for example, will take five minutes to burn. A 2x drive will burn the same five-minute song in 2½ minutes, a 4x drive in 1¼ minutes, and so on. (Note that the complete process of burning a CD will likely take slightly longer than these figures would indicate.) Each time you increase the speed you're burning at, you increase the data transfer demands on your system. A 1x audio CD requires a 172KB/sec transfer rate, a 2x, 344KB/sec, and so on. At higher speeds, writing the CD from a disc image can improve the odds of a successful burn. You might think that burning CDs at slower speeds would decrease the risk of errors, but this isn't always the case. Consult the manufacturers of your CD-burning software and hardware to determine the optimal rate for your system.

Audio CD Mastering Software

Manufacturer	Product	Price	Platform	Contact
Creative Digital Research	HyCD Play & Record	$19.95	Win	www.hycd.com
Digidesign	MasterList CD	$495	Mac	www.digidesign.com
Emagic	WaveBurner Pro	$299	Mac	www.emagic.de
Gear Software	Gear Pro	$149.95	Win	www.gearcdr.com
Golden Hawk Technology	CDR Win	$49	Win	www.goldenhawk.com
Roxio	Easy CD Creator	$99	Win	www.roxio.com
Roxio	Jam	$199	Mac	www.roxio.com
Roxio	Toast	$89	Mac	www.roxio.com
Sek'd	Red Roaster	$369	Win	www.sekd.com

added flexibility of using the significantly less expensive write-once CD-R media in addition to the CD-RW rewritable media.

CD-R drives have a read speed and a write speed. CD-RW drives have read, write, and rewrite speeds. Typical write/rewrite speeds are 1x, 2x, 4x, 8x, or even higher, while read speeds may reach 32x or greater. The faster the write speed, the faster the rest of your system needs to be (see "The Need for Speed" above).

CD-R and CD-RW drives can be connected to your computer a number of ways, including various flavors of SCSI and ATA, USB, FireWire, and parallel connections. Which one is right for you? The answer depends on your computer and your performance requirements. If you have a SCSI-based Apple Power Mac, SCSI is the obvious choice. iMacs will require a USB burner, and the latest G3s and G4s give you the option of either USB or FireWire. Most PCs have ATA (IDE) support, and many now offer USB connections, but adding a SCSI card and CD burner may provide better performance, especially if you want to burn discs at higher speeds. Avoid parallel port CD burners for audio applications.

- **Blank CD Media**

Over the past few years, lots of claims have been made about the durability and quality of various CD-R media. A good bet is to stick with the media recommended by the manufacturer of your CD burner. If you can't get a recommendation from the manufacturer, choose discs from a reliable, "name" manufacturer, and you'll be fine. With computer-based CD burners, any computer- or data-grade media should work; it's not necessary to buy special "audio" CD media.

For burning audio CDs, you're generally best off using CD-R, rather than CD-RW media, even if your drive supports CD-RW discs. Standard audio CD players won't be able to read the CD-RW discs unless you "close" the disc, which turns it into a non-rewritable CD. Since CD-R discs are much less expensive than CD-RW discs, it makes sense to use CD-R whenever the CD you're burning will need to be played in a standard audio CD player. Save the CD-RW discs for data backups and other situations where you might need to change or erase the data on the CD.

In most cases, it's not necessary to use "audio" CD-R blanks to record your music, unless your burner specifically requires them (most don't).

Burning a CD in Nine Easy Steps

1. Get your hard drive ready to go. Make sure there's sufficient space available on your hard drive to hold the audio files and disc image you'll need to burn your CD. As mentioned above, plan for 10MB per minute of CD audio—double that if you'll be using a disc image.

Consider defragmenting (optimizing) your hard drive before loading or recording audio onto it. Symantec's Norton Utilities (www.symantec.com) is one program that can help keep your hard drive operating at its best.

2. Get some audio into your computer. You can't burn an audio CD if you don't have audio files on your hard drive. You'll need to have those audio files on your drive in a format that your audio program supports. WAV files are the standard on Windows-based systems, and both AIFF or SDII (Sound Designer II) files are common on the Mac, although some CD-burning software can also create audio CDs starting from other formats, such as MP3.

Most CD-burning software has basic audio recording capabilities and can extract audio from a CD placed in the computer's CD-ROM drive. If your needs are simple, this may be all you need. We won't get into the software and hardware required to record audio on your computer in this chapter. Check out "Putting Your Studio Together" on page 37 and "Software for the Studio" on page 65 for more on this topic.

3.   Create a new session. Boot your audio CD-burning program and create a new session. Some programs default to a new session when you start the program. There's a "format" window or menu selection in most programs that tells the software what type of CD you intend to burn. Your choices may include audio CD, ISO 9660, HFS, CD-I, video CD, and others. Select audio CD.

4.   Import sound files into the session. Some programs allow you to drag and drop audio files from your computer's desktop to the session window, while others will have an Import Audio command or button used to select the audio files you want to include from your drive.

5.   Arrange the tracks in the proper order. This is usually a matter of dragging the audio files up and down in a list until you have achieved the song order you desire.

6.   Editing (optional). Some CD-burning programs allow you to edit the spacing between tracks and the volumes of the tracks, insert crossfades between tracks, and fade each track in and/or out. Other programs have default spacing between tracks that is not editable. Editing the space between tracks can make your CD sound more professional and polished. If you have a song that fades out slowly and the next song fades in slowly, a default two-second pause between tracks may seem like an eternity. Likewise, if you have a song that ends abruptly and the next one begins at full volume, you may want to adjust the space between the tracks so that your listener's brains have time to realize that the first song is over. In some cases you may not want any pause between tracks at all (usually the case with "live" or concert recordings).

Most programs will allow you to preview your tracks before you burn them to disc. It's a good idea to listen through all the transitions from track to track, and to the entire CD to make sure things flow smoothly.

7.   Load blank CD-R or CD-RW media into your CD burner.

8.   Burn the CD. Depending on the CD burner and software that you're using, you may have a choice of 1x, 2x, 4x, or faster burn speeds. You may also have the option of writing a disc image file onto your hard drive first and then burning a CD from the image file. A disc image file contains an exact representation of what the data on the final CD will look like. An image is much easier for your system to work from; it only has to open and deal with one large file, as opposed to skipping around all over your hard drive looking for and opening the various audio and data files that make up your CD.

Most programs offer a test mode where you can check to see if your system will perform the CD burn adequately before wasting your time and CD-R media doing a real burn. Let the test run long enough to ensure that things will work properly.

9. Verify the disc. When burning CD-ROMs, your computer will automatically verify that the data was written correctly to your disc. With an audio CD, you'll have to do that task manually. Listen to the CD on several different CD players. There are a variety of error correction schemes available on CD players, and occasionally an error will show up on one player but not on others.

Burning your own audio CDs can be a great way to enhance the presentation of your music. Not only are you freed from worrying about tape hiss and other problems, but your music will automatically seem more professional coming off of a CD as opposed to a hand-labeled cassette. With today's tools, it's fast and easy to create your own CDs—to say nothing of the fact that you don't have to worry about some inconsiderate oaf taping over your masterpiece. So what are you waiting for? Get burning!

preparing for CD replication

BY ROB MCGAUGHEY WITH MITCH GALLAGHER

S o your project is tracked, edited, and mixed to perfection. It's sitting in front of you on a shiny freshly burned CD-R or on a DAT tape. You've got audio examples on your Web site, and your many fans can download the music from various Internet locations. But when your followers want to purchase your album, what are you going to deliver to them? You could burn a one-off CD-R for each person who wants to buy it, but that could get just a tad tedious. Besides, CD-Rs are great, but they don't scream *professional* the way that a commercially duplicated CD does.

The solution is to send your project to a CD replicator, who will take your music and duplicate it on regular audio CDs—the same kind you buy at your friendly local CD retailer. Many musicians today are sending projects directly from their studio to the CD replicator. If you'd like to take this approach, take some time to shop for a replicator; you can find them advertising in the pages of recording magazines such as *EQ*. In addition to duplicating the CDs for you, your replicator may also be able to help you with creating CD and jewel case art, and with other aspects of giving your project a professional look and feel. The replicator can give you a complete rundown on what he can offer, as well as how you submit your project, the documentation required, etc. Here are some things to consider as you contemplate sending your CD off for duplication.

Choose the Right Media

Most CD replicators prefer to get projects on either PCM1630 tapes or CD-Rs. Since PCM1630 is far too expensive for most home or project recording studios, CD-R has become a very popular medium for submitting projects for CD replication. You should always check with the CD replicator you choose to find out their preferred media. Some replicators offer a discount for glass-ready CD-Rs. A glass-ready CD-R is a finished master that can be bit for bit replicated and contains all of the proper track indexing. Many replicators will accept projects on DAT and various other formats, but these may require CD pre-mastering to transfer them to a format that they can replicate from—which may entail extra costs.

Label Your Media

An engineer at a CD replicator may handle several projects per day and each one needs to be clearly marked. You should include band name, contact name, project title, CD replicator ID or job number, and other details pertinent to the project.

44.1kHz Sampling Frequency

This is the industry standard sampling rate for the compact disc, and it's an absolute requirement. If you send in a project at any other sampling rate it will be converted to 44.1kHz, and this conversion may cause audio degradation.

Preventive Media Maintenance

Use the highest quality media available and follow the manufacturer's requirements for maintaining. Handle CD-Rs carefully and avoid fingerprints and dust. If you are sending a project on DAT, always leave the first and last two minutes of a tape blank, as this is where most tape errors occur.

Track Sheets

Track sheets are extremely necessary documents that detail all pertinent information regarding your project. Track sheets should contain song titles, accurate song lengths (CD-Rs use CDA time, DATs use ABS time, some may offer the option of SMPTE time code), order of songs on the final master, sampling rate, brand name and model of DAT machine used to record DAT (if DAT is used), and notes for each song (such as any unusual noises and characteristics). The track sheet should be neatly typed so that it is easily read and has room for notes or highlighting by the engineer in charge of the replication. SMPTE time code is preferred on track sheets and should note frame accurate start and stop times for each song along with exact spacing times between songs.

Track Spacing

It is important to pay particular attention to track spacing. This may vary anywhere from 0 to four seconds normally but is a function of the particular tracks. A song that fades out slowly may need a shorter space before the next track, while an abrupt end to a song may require a longer pause. It is important to listen to these transitions and find the right spacing. If you default to two seconds between tracks it may seem like an eternity on some songs and feel like the two tunes run together in other places. You just have to play with track spacing until it feels right. This is an area where hard disk editors are invaluable. It is commonplace to fade to digital black (complete silence) between songs on most studio albums (this isn't true with live performances where there is usually applause between tracks). Therefore it's essential to frame-accurately note where each song starts and stops. You can cross-fade out of one song and into another without silence, but you must note that the point where song A ends and song B begins is exactly the same point. These frame-accurate times should be noted on the track sheet. A big advantage to supplying a CD-R master is that, if done properly (see "Continuous Time Code" below), it can be copied bit for bit. This allows you to control all aspects of the project including track spacing, level, and fidelity.

Levels

It is important to balance the relative volume levels from track to track. This can be done with only one instrument: the human ear. There is no meter or measuring equipment that can detect volume like the human ear, and thus it's critical to properly match levels from song to song in a manner that makes sense musically. You need to listen to the project from beginning to end and pay attention to the average loudness throughout.

Loudness is affected by processes such as compression, limiting, normalization, and also by the relatively new processors that offer loudness maximization. The trick is to use these tools to maximize the sound quality of each individual song as well as the relationship between all of the songs. There is a belief that louder is better, and this is true to a degree—listeners generally tend to perceive a louder song as sounding better—but you can easily cross a loudness threshold where the sound becomes distorted, dull, lacks stereo separation, and is lifeless and boring.

Communication

Many replicators will send out a packet of information detailing requirements, preferred formats, templates for artwork/graphics, and information on their processes. You should read this information carefully and call them if you have any questions. Some replicators have people on staff to walk you through this important process to ensure your satisfaction. You should request a test pressing and proofs to make sure that everything looks and sounds the way it should. Check every detail to make sure it's correct, and have others recheck it for you. If you don't catch problems up front you wind up with several boxes of something less than you envisioned.

Continuous Time Code

A master sent in for duplication should have continuous time code from beginning to end. This means no hitting stop or pause between tracks on your DAT or stand-alone CD recorder. This action will put digital garbage between the tracks and small gaps in the time code that will cause problems in the CD replication process. If you must use stop or pause in order to create your master then note this clearly on the track sheet, and realize that the replicator will have to digitally copy your master to another medium. This is not a big deal in most cases, but every copy of a master is an opportunity for errors—and it may add to the final cost.

Safety Copy

Never make just one safety copy. Always make at least two backups, and never send your only copy in the mail. Always listen carefully to each copy to ensure that it is error-free. Most DAT and stand-alone CD recorders output the same information as is coming in and will not allow you to hear if an error occurs on the tape/disc while recording. Therefore you must carefully listen to each copy of a tape or CD after the recording (preferably on multiple machines) and then put it away for safekeeping. Store one safety copy at a remote location in case of fire, flood, swarms of locusts, or other natural disasters.

A-weighted. A method of interpreting audio specs that accounts for our ears' frequency response.

Absorption. Using soft materials such as acoustic foam or heavy curtains to absorb audio energy. Most effective for controlling mid and high frequencies.

Absorptive material. A surface or material that converts sound waves into heat, thereby reducing the sound pressure level. While absorbers effectively control reflections in the mid-to-upper frequency ranges, they can make a room sound and feel small and overly dead. Examples include acoustic foam, ceiling tiles, and carpet.

ADSR. Attack/Decay/Sustain/Release; four-stage processor in a synthesizer or sampler that determines the volume envelope of a note.

AES/EBU. Audio Engineering Society/European Broadcast Union; protocol and connection used for digitally routing a signal from one piece of gear to another.

Ambience. The sense of "acoustic space" that surrounds a real or recorded sound.

Amplitude. Signal level.

Analog-to-digital converter (A/D). Device that converts analog voltages representing an audio signal into a digital representation of the signal.

Attack (compressor). The amount of time between the moment the signal crosses the threshold and when compression occurs. Setting a longer attack allows you to leave attack transients alone while still compressing the bulk of the signal.

Attack (noise gate). The time it takes for a noise gate to open once signal has passed the threshold. Very fast settings (10–50 microseconds) allow transients to pass accurately; slow settings (up to one second) can be used to change the attack portion of a signal's envelope.

Attack (synthesizer or sampler). The time it takes for a note to begin playing at full volume. An instrument like a drum has a fast attack, where a violin might have a slow, swelling attack.

Attenuate. Reduce the level or gain of a signal.

Audio signal. Changing voltages representing sound waves

Automation. Using computer control to change parameters on a mixer processor or other piece of gear. Allows you to very accurately perform mixdown with complete recallability.

Balanced. Type of connection that uses three wires (positive, negative, ground) to carry signal. Balanced signals provide noise cancellation, and so are generally less noisy and can be run for longer distances than unbalanced connections.

Bandwidth. Range of frequencies

Bass traps. Acoustic devices that absorb low-frequency sound waves. Bass traps can be located in the corners of a room or can be free standing. They may be necessary in situations where the room is amplifying bass frequencies.

Bit resolution. The number of bits that are available to describe an audio signal in the digital domain. As the audio level is decreased the number of bits available to describe the audio signal will decrease as well, thus reducing the integrity of the signal.

Breathing. When a large amount of compression is being applied, the noise floor will rise and fall along with the signal. You may hear this change in the noise floor in the spaces between sounds, such as between drum hits. Turning up the release time will normally solve this. See also "Pumping."

Buffer. A small amount of memory in a CD burner that's used to smooth out the data transfer rate from the computer. The size of the buffer is important to successful CD burning.

Bus. A circuit that collects audio signals and routes them to a specific destination.

Caddy. A carrier required for loading a CD into some CD-R and CD-ROM drives.

Capsule. The stage of the microphone where sound is converted into electrical signals.

CD-R. Compact Disc-Recordable, a write-once (can't be erased or modified) optical disc format.

CD-RW. Compact Disc-ReWritable, an optical disc format that allows the disc to be recorded, erased, and modified many times.

Channel. A signal path that deals with one audio signal.

Chase. To lock to, sync to, or follow timecode.

Chatter. When signal hovers around its threshold level, a gate may be unsure if it should be open or closed. It may rapidly jump back and forth, resulting in the audio cutting in and out; this is known as "chattering." To correct this problem, adjust the threshold setting slightly higher or lower, so that the input signal will more consistently drive the gate.

Chorusing. A thick, moving effect created by combining a signal with several copies of itself after time-delaying and/or pitch-shifting the copies.

Clicks. a.k.a. "ticks"; a generic term for clock pulses, the divisions between quarter-notes that a MIDI sequencer uses as a timing reference. The higher the number of pulses per quarter-note (ppq or ppqn), the more accurately the sequencer can record rhythms.

Clipping. Distortion that results from a signal being stronger than the electronics can handle. The signal above a certain level is literally clipped, or squared, off.

Comp. Short for "composite," the technique of building a single performance from pieces of several different performances. Also short for "accompany," the technique of playing chords behind a lead part.

Compressor. A processor that reduces the dynamic range of a signal.

Countermelody. An alternative melodic line played under a main melody. Unlike a harmony line, a countermelody will have its own rhythm.

Crosstalk. Amount of signal that "bleeds" through from one channel or signal path to another.

Cycles-per-second. Unit of measure for the frequency of a sound wave or audio signal.

DAT. DAT, or Digital Audio Tape, is a recording format similar to the time-honored cassette, except that the recording is done in the digital domain, so there's no hiss or loss in audio quality. DAT recorders are commonly used in pro studios for mixdown. There are also portable units available for high-quality field recording applications.

DAW. Digital Audio Workstation; stand-alone or computer-based device or collection of devices used to record, edit, mix, and process audio signals.

Decay (reverb). The time it takes the reverb to fade out. Also known as "reverb time."

Decay (synthesizer). The time it takes for an envelope to change from the attack peak level to the sustain level.

Decibel (dB). Unit of measurement for specifying the ratio of level between sounds or audio signals.

Delay time. The amount of time that elapses between the original sound and when the delayed sound is heard.

Demo. Short for "demonstration," this term refers to any rough version of a recorded musical piece.

Detector. See "Sidechain."

Diaphragm. A super-thin sheet of (usually) gold-plated Mylar within a microphone capsule that vibrates in response to sound waves. These vibrations are converted into electrical currents by the capsule.

Diffusion (acoustics). Using staggered or angled surfaces to break up and scatter audio reflections into a room.

Diffusion (reverb). Parameter that determines how dense or "thick" a reverb sounds. Also known as "density."

Digital-to-analog converter (D/A). Device that changes a digital representation of a signal into an analog voltage.

Direct box (DI). Device used to convert high-impedance signals to low-impedance.

Disc-at-once. A write mode in which an entire CD is written in one pass, without turning off the write laser. Disc-at-once writing prevents certain errors on the CD that can be a problem if it will be sent to a replicator for mass duplication.

Distortion. Unwanted (normally) change in the waveform of a sound.

Doubling. A term that comes from double-tracking; a process of overdubbing two takes of the same part onto separate tracks and mixing them together. Since the two performances aren't quite identical, all sorts of timing and harmonic relationships exist that create a thicker, fuller, and more interesting sound. With effects processors, doubling is created with short delay times (10–50 ms) in an attempt to achieve similar results. With doubling, the delay is so short that (except with percussive source material) it can't be heard as a distinct repeat or echo.

Dry. Unprocessed.

Dynamic range. The difference between a signal's loudest and softest levels, or the range of levels a piece of gear is capable of reproducing without distortion. The difference between the noise floor and the onset of distortion.

Early reflections (reverb). The closely spaced echoes created when an acoustic sound reaches the listener's ears after bouncing off nearby walls. Also, the parameter used in a reverb algorithm to mimic the effect of such echoes.

Early reflection (acoustics). The first audio reflections to arrive at the listener's ear (or microphone) after the original source sound is heard. Early reflections interfere with the original sound and must be controlled for accurate monitoring or recording.

Echo. A signal delayed by a long enough time that it can be heard as a distinctly separate event is sometimes called echo. More often, however, it's simply called delay.

Equalizer (EQ). Audio processor that allows the level or gain of specific frequencies to be increased or decreased. Used to adjust the tone or timbral balance of a signal.

Expander. The opposite of a compressor; a device used to increase the dynamic range of a signal. In an expander, the level of the output signal is increased based on a ratio applied to the input signal. with a 1:2 ratio, a change of 1dB at the expander input results in a change of 2dB at its output. Downward expanders are most often used like noise gates to control the amount of background noise in a signal path.

Fader. A sliding volume control used to vary signal level.

First reflection. The first reflection of a sound off a surface that arrives at the listener's ear after the original source sound is heard. First reflections interfere with the original sound and must be controlled for accurate monitoring.

Flutter, flutter echo. An acoustic anomaly caused by a sound wave bouncing quickly between two parallel surfaces. The resulting effect is a very short "rattling" type of echo often described as fluttering.

Frame rate. The speed of the timecode, usually expressed in frames per second (fps). A number of rates are in common use, including 25, 29.97 drop frame, and 30 fps. If you're working with clients or other studios, make sure you all use the same frame rate. Otherwise, choose a rate and stick to it. Note that the frame rate is not related to the tempo of your music. Rather, it's a timing constant for the synced gear to refer to.

Freewheel. Some timecode readers can continue playing even if they lose the incoming timecode signal. This is called "freewheeling."

Frequency. Rate at which a sound wave is vibrating.

Frequency response. The range of frequencies a piece of gear can respond to.

Frequency response curve. A representation of how well a device responds to those frequencies it can reproduce. The flatter the response curve of a device is, the more evenly it handles the range of frequencies it reproduces.

Gain. Signal strength or level.

Gain staging. Setting up the gain or level at various points in a signal path for optimum performance.

Gate. See "Noise gate."

General MIDI (GM). An industry standard that aims to make it easy to transfer a MIDI song from one system to another. If a synth is GM-compatible, it uses a certain order for its patches (*e.g.,* patch one is always a piano), it has 24 notes of polyphony, and so on.

Hard knee. Full compression is applied as soon as the signal crosses the threshold. See also "Soft knee."

Haas effect. A psychoacoustic phenomenon in which delay creates an apparent change in left/right stereo balance in a signal. When an identical signal is sent to the left and right channels at the same volume, but one side is delayed by a few milliseconds, our ears perceive the sound as coming from the side that arrives earlier. The strength of the effect depends on the amount of delay.

Headroom. Dynamic range available between normal operating level and the onset of clipping or distortion. Headroom becomes important when dealing with combining signal levels or signals that have widely changing levels.

Hertz. Cycles per second; a unit of measure for the frequency of a sound wave or signal.

Hold. The amount of time a gate will stay fully open after its input signal falls below the threshold. Common settings range from two milliseconds to two seconds.

Image. A file that contains an exact representation of the data that will be written to a CD. If you have a slow hard drive or computer, when burning CDs at higher speeds (*i.e.,* 4x, 8x) it's best to do so from an image file rather than from the raw data.

Jam sync. The ability of a timecode device to generate new timecode while it's receiving old timecode. This capability is used to replace old timecode if it's been damaged or is becoming corrupted.

Key input. See "Sidechain."

Lock. To slave to timecode or clock signals. A device is "locked" when it sees and is completely synced to the timecode signal. Some devices require a short "pre-roll" period in order to get up to speed and to lock to timecode each time they're played.

Loop. A short segment of audio, such as a measure of a drum beat, that's repeated to provide rhythmic backing for a piece of music. A loop can also be created from non-rhythmic material for sustaining or textural effects.

LTC (Linear Time Code). Timecode (usually SMPTE) represented as a continuous stream of signal on a linear track.

Limiter. A compressor with a very high ratio; typically used to establish a ceiling level above which signals aren't allowed to pass.

Makeup gain. The amount of volume or level increase applied to the signal at the final output stage of a compressor. This allows you to compensate for volume lost in the compression process.

Master. The device that's generating or playing back the sync information for a system.

MDM. Modular Digital Multitrack; multitrack recorders designed to be easily synced or locked together to provide more tracks.

Modulation. A change (either in a signal or in the value of a parameter in a device) that occurs in real time, as the signal is passing through the device.

MIDI. Musical Instrument Digital Interface; protocol that allows various pieces of music and audio gear to communicate with and control each other.

MIDI Time Code (MTC). A version of LTC carried over MIDI.

Millisecond (ms). One-thousandth of a second.

Mixdown. The process of combining and processing individual tracks or signals into a cohesive final form.

Mixer. A device that is used to combine and manipulate multiple audio signals.

Mono or Monophonic. An audio signal consisting of one channel of information.

Multi-tap delay. A type of stereo delay with multiple delay occurrences at user-determined intervals. There can be from two to 20 or more taps available, each with its own delay time, output level, panning, and (often) feedback amount.

Multitrack. A recorder that is capable of recording and playing many independent signals simultaneously.

Mute. To turn off an audio signal or channel, or a control that allows you to turn off a signal or channel.

Noise. An unwanted audio signal, such as rumble, hiss, or hum.

Noise floor. The level of background noise produced by a piece of audio gear.

Noise gate. Processor that automatically shuts off a channel when no desired signal is present.

Note stealing. What happens when you exceed the maximum polyphony of a synth module by trying to play too many notes at once. Some notes don't get played, or are cut off early. Their polyphony is "stolen" so that other notes can sound.

Off-axis. Entering a microphone from somewhere other than directly in front of the diaphragm.

On-axis. Entering a microphone from directly in front of the diaphragm.

Overdub. Track that is recorded, or the process of recording a track, after the original (basic) tracks have been recorded.

Pad. A circuit or processor that attenuates (reduces the level of) signals to prevent subsequent circuitry from distorting in high-volume situations.

Pan or panoramic potentiometer. Control that varies the balance of signal level in multiple output channels.

Panning. Moving a signal to the left or right in the stereo field.

Phase cancellation. The result of summing (mixing) two identical sound waves that are out of phase with one another. Phase cancellation can cause a serious loss of level as well as a noticeable change in the timbre or tone of the resulting signal.

Ping-pong delay. A type of echo effect in which a repeating delayed sound alternates between the left and right channels of a stereo image.

Plosive. A vocal sound that creates a burst of air, which is interpreted by microphones as a "pop"; *p's* and *b's* are plosives.

Pocket. In all forms of music, but especially in jazz and funk, that place where an instrument sits most comfortably in the rhythm. Sometimes found slightly ahead of the beat, sometimes a bit behind, the pocket is where a part simply "feels" best.

Polar pattern. A representation of how a microphone responds to audio signals entering it from various directions.

Polyphony. The number of notes a keyboard or sound module can play at once. See also "Note stealing."

Portable mix. A mix that sounds pretty much the same when played on systems other than the studio monitors it was mixed on.

Post-fader send. A bus that occurs after the channel faders. Post-fader send levels are affected by moving the channel fader; they're usually used as effects sends.

Predelay. The length of time between the initial signal and the onset of reverb.

Pre-fader send. A bus occurring before the channel fader. Pre-fader sends aren't affected by the level the faders are set at—the fader can be moved without changing the send level—and are therefore often used for monitor and headphone feeds.

Program change. MIDI signal that tells the receiving device to change the preset or program it is using.

Psychoacoustic. Effects caused by the brain being tricked into misinterpreting sonic cues (*e.g.,* diffusors that make a room seem larger than it actually is).

Pumping. If a compressor's release time is too long, signals below the threshold may still be compressed, pushing them down in the mix, then slowly letting them rise up to their normal level. Shorten release time to correct this. See also "Breathing."

Punch-in. The technique of replacing small portions of a take by "punching" your recorder or sequencer in and out of record for just long enough to fix a mistake.

Quantizing. A feature of MIDI sequencers that automatically lines up MIDI events to a timing grid (for example, to the nearest eighth-note). Useful for producing a mechanized feel, or for correcting a rhythmically sloppy performance.

RAM. Random Access Memory; a type of computer memory chip that that can both be read and written to.

Random access. Ability to access information in a non-linear fashion.

Ratio. The amount of compression that is applied when the signal is above the threshold. Ratio refers to the change in output level for a given input level change: With a 2:1 ratio, a 2dB change in input level results in a 1dB change in output level. A higher ratio (*e.g.,* 2:1, 3:1, 10:1) increases the amount of compression applied to the signal. A limiter will exhibit a very high ratio, 10:1 or even

higher, effectively creating a maximum level above which the signal is prevented from going.

Red Book. A specification developed by Sony and Philips for the audio CD format.

Regeneration. A setting on a delay unit that determines how many times a delayed sound repeats before it fades out. Also known as feedback.

Release (compressor). The amount of time that passes between when the input signal to a compressor drops below its threshold and when the unit is no longer applying compression.

Release (noise gate). The time it takes for a gate to decay or close after the hold stage is complete. Common settings range from 2ms to four seconds.

Release (synthesizer or sampler). The amount of time a sound continues playing after a note has been stopped or key let up.

Return. An input connection used to bring a signal back into a mixer after it has been processed.

Reverb. Multiple echoes that blend together in an acoustic space such as a concert hall. The sound of reverb gives the listener important information about the size and shape of the space in which the sound is being played. A type of signal processing (typically digital these days) that produces a continuous wash of echoing sound. Reverberation contains the same frequency components as the sound being processed, but no discrete echoes.

ROM. Read Only Memory; computer memory chip whose contents can only be read, not modified or replaced by the user.

Sample. A single digital snapshot of an audio signal.

Sample rate. The speed at which samples are taken by a digital device. Usually specified in samples/second or kilo-Hertz (kHz). The sample rate determines the frequency response of the digital signal.

Scratch. A rough version; a scratch track or scratch vocal is there for reference and will eventually be replaced.

Self-noise. The amount of background noise generated by a microphone's electronics.

Send. A bus, separate from the main mix, usually routed to a processor or to monitors or headphones.

Sensitivity. How much voltage a microphone produces for a given audio level. Measured in millivolts per Pascal (mV/Pa; a Pascal is a unit of sound pressure level).

Sequencer. A device or computer program that can record, generate, edit, modify, and play back MIDI information.

Sibilance. High frequency, airy vocal sounds such as *ss* and *sh*.

Sidechain. An input used to control a compressor or noise gate's operation. Signal present at the sidechain input is not heard through the unit's audio path; it's used to control when the unit is processing the audio path.

Signal-to-noise ratio. The difference between a device's noise floor and its nominal, or normal, operating level.

Slapback. A type of delay where only a single delay repeat is heard, and the delayed sound is nearly the same volume as the original. Slapback delay times are generally short, around 80–150ms.

Slave. To follow, sync to, lock to, or chase a master sync device. Also the device that's chasing the master device.

SMPTE. Society of Motion Picture and Television Engineers; also the name of a common form of linear timecode (LTC).

Soft knee. Compression is applied gradually as the signal crosses the threshold. In general, soft knee compression is less noticable, especially at higher compression ratios.

Solo. A switch that allows the engineer to monitor, or listen to, only the selected channel.

S/PDIF. Sony/Philips Digital Interface; protocol and connection used for digitally routing a signal from one piece of gear to another.

SPL. Sound Pressure Level.

Standing wave. A sound wave that reflects back and forth in a room because its wavelength is a multiple of the distance between two hard parallel surfaces. Because the reflections are in phase, this creates a boost or ringing at that frequency.

Stereo. An audio signal consisting of two channels of related information.

Stereo link. A means of connecting the operation of two channels, turning a processor with two independent channels into a true stereo device. When engaged, a stereo link switch will trigger both the left and right channels of a compressor whenever a signal crosses the threshold in either channel. This maintains the integrity of the stereo field and the location of items placed within it.

Stripe. The process of recording timecode onto a track of a recorder.

Sustain (synthesizer). The level at which a note plays after the attack and decay, while the key is held down.

Sweet spot. The area in a studio generally defined as the most accurate physical location from which to listen to the monitors.

Sync. To lock the rates or speeds of multiple devices together.

Threshold (compressor). The loudness level at which compression begins to occur. The threshold control on your compressor allows you to adjust the level above which the processing will be triggered. Compression only occurs on signals above the threshold; those below the threshold are passed unaltered.

Threshold (gate). Input level at which a gate opens. The trick is to accurately set the threshold control so that background noise is gated, but desired signal is allowed to pass through without being chopped off. In general, set the threshold just barely high enough to remove unwanted noise.

Ticks. See "Clicks."

Timbre. Tonal quality.

Timecode. A signal containing timing/location information.

Time compression/time expansion. Processing applied to audio files to change their tempo without changing their pitch. Many software packages can do this—the trick is to do it without changing the audio quality or timbre of the sound.

TOC (Table of Contents). An area on a CD that contains information on the number of tracks on the disc, their start locations, and so on.

Track-at-once. A CD write mode that allows you to add data to a disc one track at a time.

Tracking. The process of recording the individual parts that will make up a piece of music.

Transducer. A device that converts one form of energy into another. Examples include microphones, speakers, guitar pickups, etc.

Transient. A quick "spike" in an audio signal. The attack of a piano note, a drum hit, and the "pluck" portion of a guitar note are all examples of transients.

Trigger. see "Sidechain."

Trim. A control that determines the initial level of signal in a mixer or other piece of gear.

Tube. an electronic component used to amplify a signal. Because of the way they work, tubes often add a pleasant, desirable distortion to signals they process, interpreted as "warmth."

Unbalanced. Type of connection that uses two wires (hot and ground) to carry signal. Unbalanced signals don't provide noise cancellation, and are therefore susceptible to picking up noise and interference. In general, unbalanced connections should be kept as short as possible, and should not be run for longer than 30 feet.

Valve. British term for tube.

VITC (Vertical Interval Time Code). Timecode information generally used in the film/video/broadcast realms. VITC is written into the frames of the video signal, rather than recorded to a linear audio track. Its advantage is that the timecode information can be read while playback is stopped, unlike LTC, which can only be read during playback.

VU (Volume Unit) meter. A mechanical device that gives a readout of average signal strength. Most VU meters don't respond well to transients.

Wavelength. Literally, a measure of how long a sound wave is. The lower the frequency, the longer the wave will be.

Wet. Processed by an effect processor.

Wet/dry mix. The parameter that controls the relative levels of the uneffected (dry) versus the processed (wet) signal output by an effects device.

Word clock. High-resolution synchronization signal used to control the sample rate of a piece of digital gear.

ABOUT THE AUTHOR/EDITOR

itch Gallagher has been recording music since he encountered his first four-track cassette recorder in 1982. An award-winning composer, Gallagher studied music composition, recording, and classical and electric guitar at Moorhead State University in Moorhead, Minnesota, continuing with graduate school studies at the University of Missouri, Kansas City.

Along with years of work in pro audio retail and as a freelance recording and live sound engineer, Gallagher has taught college-level recording and electronic music classes and labs, numerous music store seminars on recording, MIDI, and live sound, and lectured on those topics both in the United States and in Europe.

As a guitarist, he toured the Midwest for several years; then he began assembling his first project studio, which grew through many incarnations into MAG Media Productions, a full-service studio offering recording, mixing, editing, mastering, radio and multimedia production, and more.

In 1998 he was named the Technical Editor at *Keyboard* magazine, where he also edited the magazine version of *Make Music Now!* In 2000 Gallagher was named the Editor of *EQ* magazine. He currently resides in New York City, where he is in the midst of work on an album of his fingerstyle acoustic guitar instrumentals. He can be emailed at mitch_gallagher@hotmail.com.

Serious Players.

The Music Player Network is for serious players. From guitars, bass, keyboards and recording to computer music culture, dance, trance and more. • Our industry-leading magazines, *Guitar Player*, *Keyboard*, *Bass Player*, *Gig*, *MC²*, *Rumble*, *EQ* and *Extreme Groove*, take the art of playing music seriously. And so does our leading portal website, MusicPlayer.com. • Our editors and writers are experienced musicians and engineers with special insights and hands-on experience that only comes from real-time playing. • If you want to get serious about your playing, check us out at your nearest newsstand or visit MusicPlayer.com on the web.

Influence.

Photo:
(left to right, top to bottom)

George Massenburg,
Ed Cherney,
Roger Nichols,
Craig Anderton,
Chris Stone
and Al Kooper.

EQ

Magazine and Forums
MusicPlayer.com:
ere our influence works for you.

These industry leaders are regular contributors to EQ magazine and the highly popular EQ Expert Forums on MusicPlayer.com. The world's largest audience of buyers of recording and sound gear depend on them for expert advice.

EQ readers and Forum regulars are recording professionals with open minds about your brands and products who are constantly looking for new tools, techniques and creative solutions to make the best possible recordings.

EQ. The expert publication of influence in recording.

For more about EQ, please call Adam Cohen at 310-313-4200 or email acohen@uemedia.com.

WHEN IT COMES TO MUSIC, WE WROTE THE BOOK.